Java Memory Management

A comprehensive guide to garbage collection and JVM tuning

Maaike van Putten

Seán Kennedy

BIRMINGHAM—MUMBAI

Java Memory Management

Copyright © 2022 Packt Publishing

Group Product Manager: Gebin George

Publishing Product Manager: Kunal Sawant

Senior Editor: Rounak Kulkarni

Technical Editor: Jubit Pincy

Copy Editor: Safis Editing

Language Support Editor: Safis Editing

Project Coordinator: Deeksha Thakkar

Proofreader: Safis Editing

Indexer: Hemangini Bari

Production Designer: Shankar Kalbhor

Developer Relations Marketing Executive: Sonakshi Bubbar

Business Development Executive: Kriti Sharma

First published: November 2022

Production reference: 1281022

Published by Packt Publishing Ltd.

Livery Place

35 Livery Street

Birmingham

B3 2PB, UK.

ISBN 978-1-80181-285-6

www.packt.com

To my students and my teachers.

– Maaike van Putten

To my wife, Maria, and my daughters, Emily, Miriam, and Lilian.

– Seán Kennedy

Contributors

About the authors

Maaike van Putten is an experienced software developer and trainer with a passion for software development and helping others to get to the next level in their career. Some of her favorite languages are Java, JavaScript, and Python. She participates as a developer in software development projects and teaches a lot of training courses, ranging from IT for beginners to advanced topics for senior software developers. She also loves to create online content to help a larger audience, and she does so for diverse platforms such as Pluralsight, LinkedIn Learning, and Udemy.

I want to thank my students, my teachers, my friends, and my family for always supporting me.

Seán Kennedy is a university lecturer with over 20 years of experience in teaching. He has a PhD in IT and is Oracle-certified in Java at the Professional level (OCP). In his daily work, he teaches Java on a bespoke master's program for a highly regarded software company. He has a YouTube channel called *Let's Get Certified* that teaches Java at all levels and prepares candidates for Java certification. He also has similar courses on Udemy. Outside of work, he enjoys tennis, walking, nature, reading, and TV.

I want to thank the people who have always supported me, especially my wife, Maria, and my late parents.

About the reviewers

Himanshu Agrawal is an industry veteran with close to 13 years of experience in designing and implementing solutions in JEE technologies. Currently, he works as an Associate Consultant with CGI, with whom he has been associated for close to 13 years. Himanshu specializes in niche technical areas like JVM, Multithreading, TLS, and Apache HTTPD. He is an Oracle Certified Java Dev, Oracle Certified Web Component Dev and certified by Google Cloud in Architecting with Google Kubernetes Engine. Moreover, he is a Certified SAFe 5 Practitioner and has done certificate courses from top universities like Harvard (via HarvardX) and MIT (via MITx). Himanshu extends his technical expertise to teams primarily in BFSI and Telecom sectors.

Silviu Turuga is an IT professional who has worked for almost 20 years for different companies around the world. During this time, he has performed various roles, from technical support, software development, and technical team lead to DevOps and DevSecOps. He has used many different programming languages and frameworks. Silviu is an Oracle Certified Professional for Java 8. He loves to see everything as a challenge that has to have a solution. He is an active team player, willing to share his knowledge with others, and also enjoys mentoring. During his free time, he likes to perform home automation and play with IoT devices.

Table of Contents

Preface

Understanding how Java memory works can be of great benefit to your Java coding and application management. It makes it easier to visualize what is going on with object composition and what happens with object allocation and deallocation, combined with object composition. As you are probably aware, object composition is where objects contain other objects. For example, a `Person` class specifies a property of type `Address`, which also happens to be a class. Knowing how this all works in memory makes it easier to know what steps to take to get to a certain data field.

Also, the concept of `static` and accessing the instance using the `this` keyword will be so much easier to visualize and understand completely when you understand how the memory of Java works. Without understanding how Java memory works, it is impossible to truly grasp the concepts of `static` and `this`.

Another advantage of understanding Java memory well is that the difference between using a primitive or a class reference as an argument makes a lot more sense all of a sudden. This also helps with understanding the immutability and mutability of objects.

More complex topics will make more sense too, such as **concurrency**, one of my personal favorites. This is when multiple things are happening at the same time in your application (multithreading). It's possible that you haven't worked with it yet, but as a Java developer, you'll have to one day. Understanding Java memory makes it easier to understand certain aspects of concurrency, especially data access. Another complex topic that will be easier to understand is garbage collection. This is of crucial importance for performance since it's a very expensive process, and you want to need it as little as possible and optimize it as much as possible.

Everything that you are probably using on a daily basis already will become clearer when you understand better how Java memory works.

Who this book is for

This book is for all sorts of Java professionals. It doesn't really matter whether you're a junior or senior developer, a DevOps engineer, a tester, or the system admin of a Java application. If you currently do not have an in-depth knowledge of Java memory, garbage collection, and/or JVM tuning, this book will help you to take your Java skills to the next level.

What this book covers

Chapter 1, Different Parts of Java Memory, covers the different parts of Java memory: the stack, the heap, and the Metaspace. We'll start with the stack memory and how variables are stored on the stack. We'll then move on to deal with objects and how these are stored on the heap. Next, we'll briefly discuss accessing primitives and objects. Finally, we'll describe the Metaspace and what it's used for.

Chapter 2, Primitives and Objects in Java Memory, zooms in on primitives and objects in Java memory. We'll be dealing with the heap and stack in more detail here. With the use of visualization, we'll show what happens during the execution of a Java program with the stack and the heap memory. Once the basics of memory management are clear, we'll deal with object references in more detail. We explain how Java's call-by-value mechanism, when applied to references, can lead to a security issue known as **escaping references**. We discuss how to solve this issue.

Chapter 3, Zooming in on the Heap Space, focuses on the different parts of the heap space. It has two main areas: the young generation space and the tenured space. The young generation space contains two separate areas: the eden space and the survivor space. We won't dive into the garbage collection process in this chapter, but we'll briefly mention it and what it is to explain how objects are promoted between spaces. Visualization of the heap and the different areas will be added to provide clarity regarding the heap space's details. The content of this chapter is necessary to understand the garbage collection algorithms that will be discussed in the next chapter.

Chapter 4, Freeing the Memory with Garbage Collection, dives into the deallocation of the objects on the heap. Deallocation of the memory is necessary in order for an application to keep running. Without the ability to free memory, we could allocate it only once and eventually we'd run out of memory. In this chapter, we are dealing with when objects on the heap space are eligible for garbage collection and what phases the garbage collector goes through. We'll end with a discussion on the different implementations of the garbage collector. We'll make this as visual as possible to increase understanding.

Chapter 5, Zooming in on the Metaspace, touches upon the Metaspace, which is used by the JVM for class metadata and for example static variables. This metadata gets stored when the classes are loaded. We'll describe the class loading process and how memory is allocated. The releasing of Metaspace memory is a bit different from the releasing of heap memory. This process will be described here as well.

Chapter 6, Configuring and Monitoring the Memory Management of the JVM, explains how to get started with JVM tuning. First, we'll describe what JVM tuning is and who needs it. There are several metrics that are relevant for the tuning of the JVM when it comes to memory management. We'll examine these metrics and how to obtain them. We'll end with the actual tuning and adjusting of the configuration of the JVM and how to use profiling to get insights into the effects of the tuning.

Chapter 7, Avoiding Memory Leaks, deals with how to use the memory well and how to spot and solve memory leaks. Whenever objects are held in memory that are no longer needed, we get memory leaks. In the beginning, this can seem harmless, but over time it will slow down an application and the application will require a restart in order to function properly again. In this chapter, we're going to make sure that the reader understands memory leaks and knows how to spot them. We'll end with very common mistakes that lead to memory leaks and how to avoid them.

To get the most out of this book

This book assumes Java 8 or later. A particular operating system or IDE is not mandatory. If you plan to run the examples yourself, then VisualVM, the visual tool for monitoring Java applications in memory, would be useful.

If you currently have nothing installed on your system, the following setup will suffice:

- JDK 8 or later (Oracle's JDK or OpenJDK)
- IntelliJ IDEA(community edition is good enough) or Eclipse
- VisualVM

Software/hardware covered in the book	Operating system requirements
Java 8+	Windows, macOS, or Linux

If you are using the digital version of this book, we advise you to type the code yourself or access the code from the book's GitHub repository (a link is available in the next section). Doing so will help you avoid any potential errors related to the copying and pasting of code.

Download the example code files

You can download the example code files for this book from GitHub at `https://github.com/PacktPublishing/B18762_Java-Memory-Management`. If there's an update to the code, it will be updated in the GitHub repository.

We also have other code bundles from our rich catalog of books and videos available at `https://github.com/PacktPublishing/`. Check them out!

Download the color images

We also provide a PDF file that has color images of the screenshots and diagrams used in this book. You can download it here: `https://packt.link/OeQqF`.

Conventions used

There are a number of text conventions used throughout this book.

`Code in text`: Indicates code words in text, database table names, folder names, filenames, file extensions, pathnames, dummy URLs, user input, and Twitter handles. Here is an example: "For example, `int x;` defines (creates) a primitive variable x which is of (the primitive) type `int`."

A block of code is set as follows:

```
Object o = new Object();
System.out.println(o);
o = null;
```

When we wish to draw your attention to a particular part of a code block, the relevant lines or items are set in bold:

```
Object o = new Object();
System.out.println(o);
o = null;
```

Any command-line input or output is written as follows:

```
java.lang.Object@4617c264
```

Bold: Indicates a new term, an important word, or words that you see on screen. For instance, words in menus or dialog boxes appear in **bold**. Here is an example: "There is a **Create another** option beside the **Create** button."

> **Tips or important notes**
> Appear like this.

Get in touch

Feedback from our readers is always welcome.

General feedback: If you have questions about any aspect of this book, email us at `customercare@packtpub.com` and mention the book title in the subject of your message.

Errata: Although we have taken every care to ensure the accuracy of our content, mistakes do happen. If you have found a mistake in this book, we would be grateful if you would report this to us. Please visit `www.packtpub.com/support/errata` and fill in the form.

Piracy: If you come across any illegal copies of our works in any form on the internet, we would be grateful if you would provide us with the location address or website name. Please contact us at copyright@packt.com with a link to the material.

If you are interested in becoming an author: If there is a topic that you have expertise in and you are interested in either writing or contributing to a book, please visit authors.packtpub.com.

Share Your Thoughts

Once you've read *Java Memory Management*, we'd love to hear your thoughts! Scan the QR code below to go straight to the Amazon review page for this book and share your feedback.

https://packt.link/r/1801812853

Your review is important to us and the tech community and will help us make sure we're delivering excellent quality content.

Download a Free PDF copy of this book

Thanks for purchasing this book!

Do you like to read on the go but are unable to carry your print books everywhere?

Is your eBook purchase not compatible with the device of your choice?

Don't worry, now with every Packt book you get a DRM-free PDF version of that book at no cost.

Read anywhere, any place, on any device. Search, copy, and paste code from your favorite technical books directly into your application.

The perks don't stop there, you can get exclusive access to discounts, newsletters, and great free content in your inbox daily

Follow these simple steps to get the benefits:

1. Scan the QR code or visit the link below

https://packt.link/free-ebook/9781801812856

2. Submit your proof of purchase
3. That's it! We'll send your free PDF and other benefits to your email directly

1
Different Parts of the Java Memory

Do you know the phenomenon of having to restart an application to boost the performance of that application? If so, you may have experienced the outcome of poor **memory management**: the memory getting full and the application slowing down. This is not always why applications slow down – other causes such as processing data from a server or a bottleneck in the network, among other things, play a role – but memory management problems are a usual suspect of degrading application performance.

You've probably heard of memory in the field of computer science before. That makes sense because computers have memory and they use this memory to store and access data while running programs (which in their turn are data too!).

So, when does an application use memory? Well, for example, let's say you'd like to run an application that is going to process a huge video file. If you do this with your activity monitoring application (for example, Activity Monitor on macOS or Task Manager on Windows) open, you'll see that the used memory increases once you open the application and load the video. Memory is a finite resource on your computer and once your computer runs out of it, it becomes slow.

There are many ways to improve the performance of an application. A deeper understanding of how exactly this memory works is one of the ways that could help you improve the performance of your applications. Memory that is used efficiently by using good practices in coding is going to boost the performance of your application. So, coding well and being mindful of how the memory works should always be the first way to achieve high performance when it comes to memory management. There is another way in which Java memory management can be influenced and that is by configuring the **Java Virtual Machine (JVM)**, which takes care of the **Java memory**. This is something that we'll cover in *Chapter 6* when we're ready for it.

The efficient handling of Java memory is of crucial importance for the performance of a Java application. In Java, this is especially the case because it comes with expensive processes such as garbage collection, which again, we'll see later after gaining enough basic knowledge to comprehend it.

Memory management is also important for data integrity in a concurrent context. Don't worry if this sounds very complicated at the moment. By the end of this book, you'll understand what is meant by this.

So, to optimize the usage of our application's Java memory, we'll first need to understand what this memory looks like and gain knowledge of the basic processes with the memory. In this chapter, we'll do just that. We're going to explore the different parts of Java memory and how we use this in our day-to-day coding. You'll get a good overview of Java memory and you'll be ready for the deep dive that's coming in the next chapters. In order to do so, we'll cover the following topics:

- Understanding computer memory and Java memory
- Creating variables in Java
- Storing variables on the stack
- Creating objects in Java
- Storing objects on the heap
- Exploring the Metaspace

Technical requirements

The code for this chapter can be found on GitHub at `PacktPublishing/B18762_Java-Memory-Management`.

Understanding computer memory and Java memory

First things first – running applications, Java or not, requires computer memory. The application's memory is the physical memory of the computer. Having more knowledge about the memory of the computer is going to help in our understanding of Java memory. Therefore, let's discuss the concept of memory and Java memory in a bit more detail.

Computer memory

Chances are that you already know this, but just to reiterate: a computer has memory. This is the part of the computer that is used for storing information that is used for executing processes. We also call this the main memory or sometimes primary storage. An important point to make here is that this is different from computer storage, where long-term information is stored. This storage is long-term because the HDD storage stores the information magnetically and the SDD can be qualified as **Electrically Erasable Programmable Read-Only Memory (EEPROM)**. They don't need constant power to persist the data. On the other hand, one common type of main memory, **Random Access Memory (RAM)**, needs constant electricity power to persist data.

This can be compared to our human brains, at least partially. We have long-term and short-term memory. We use our long-term memory for our, well, memories – for example, a cherished childhood memory of your father pushing you around playfully in a wheelbarrow while your mother quoted from your most beloved storybook while you were wearing your favorite outfit that you had as a 3-year-old (magical, let's save the rest for my memoir or therapist). Then there's short-term memory, which is great when you want to remember the six digits for a two-step verification process and even better if you can't recall them a few minutes later.

Accessing the main memory

The computer, or actually the CPU of the computer, can access the main memory much faster than it can access the permanent storage space. In the main memory, programs are currently open and the data that they're using is being stored.

Maybe you can recall starting your computer and opening an app you use daily for the first time that day and realizing that it takes a few seconds to boot. If you close it, perhaps accidentally, and open it again right after closing it, it is a lot faster. The main memory works as some sort of cache or buffer, and this explains the phenomenon of the shorter load time the second time. The second time, it can open it from the main memory instead of from the storage, which proves, or at least supports, the point that the main memory is faster.

The great news is that you don't need to understand the tiniest details of the computer memory, but a rough overview will help.

Overview of the main memory

The most common part of the main memory is the RAM. The RAM is a huge part of what determines the performance of a computer. Running or active applications need RAM for storing and accessing data. This memory can be accessed very quickly by the applications and processes. If there is enough RAM available and if the **Operating System (OS)** does a great job of managing the RAM, your applications will reach their performance potential.

You can see how much RAM is available by having a look at your monitoring app. For me, that is Activity Monitor. As you can see in the following figure, my computer is using quite a bit of memory at the moment:

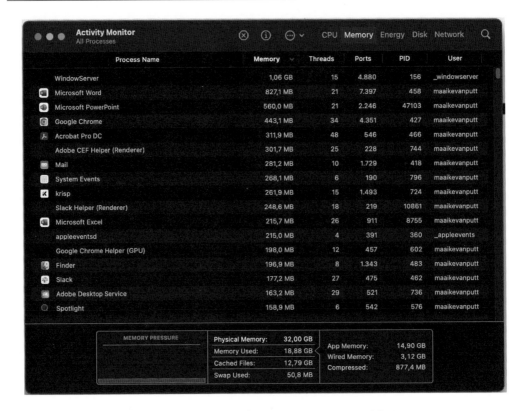

Figure 1.1 – Screenshot of Activity Monitor on macOS 12.5

I have sorted the processes from high memory to low. At the bottom, you can see a summary of the available memory and the memory used. To be honest, this seems a little high and I should probably investigate it after writing this chapter.

Why should I investigate this if I still have a lot of memory available? Well, if the RAM gets too full, the applications that are running can only do so very slowly. This is something you're likely to have experienced already when you've run more or heavier applications than your computer specifications allowed.

The RAM is volatile. This means that when you turn off the power, the information is gone. The main memory does not only consist of RAM. The **Read-Only Memory** (**ROM**) is part of the main memory too, but it's non-volatile. It contains instructions that the computer needs to start, so luckily this does not disappear when we turn the power off!

> **Fun fact**
>
> We refer to the main memory as RAM, which is very common terminology, but now you know it's technically incorrect! A fun fact indeed.

Java memory and the JVM

You may wonder if we are still going to cover Java memory – and yes, we are! The Java memory is somewhat similar to, but also different from, the computer's memory model. However, before we talk about Java memory, I'll need to explain what the JVM is. I really appreciate your patience, I must say.

The JVM

The JVM executes Java applications. Does that mean that the JVM understands Java? No, not at all! It understands bytecode – the `.class` files. This means the compiled Java programs. The code of some other languages, such as **Kotlin**, is compiled to JVM bytecode as well and can therefore be interpreted by the JVM. This is why they're sometimes referred to as JVM languages, such as Java, Kotlin, and Scala, among others.

The steps can be seen in *Figure 1.2*:

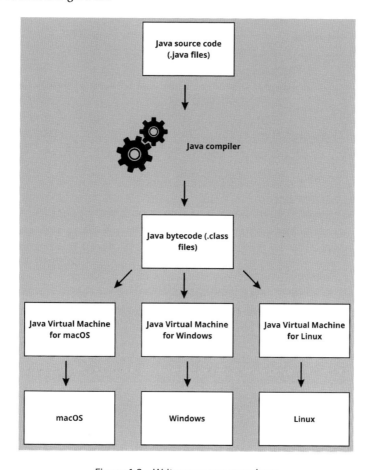

Figure 1.2 – Write once, run anywhere

The source code (in the figure, we assume this is Java source code) is being compiled by the Java compiler. The result is .class files containing bytecode. This bytecode can be interpreted by the JVM. Every platform, whether macOS, Windows, or Linux, has its own version of the JVM to execute the bytecode. This means that the application doesn't need to be modified to run on different environments because the platform-specific JVM takes care of that.

The JVM is actually why Java once was famous and beloved for its *write once, run anywhere* principle. The reason Java is not so famous for this anymore is that it's sort of normal for languages to work this way nowadays. Any platform with a JVM installed on it could run Java since the JVM takes care of translating it to the machine it's running on.

I typically compare this to a travel plug adapter. Plugs don't fit globally because different regions use different sockets. You can use your own adapter wherever you are when you have the right travel adapter plug with you. In this case, the travel adapter would be the JVM. The *"wherever you are"* would be the platform you're trying to run Java on and your adapter would be your Java program.

Let's see the basics of how the JVM deals with memory management.

Memory management and the JVM

The Java memory stores the data that is required to run Java applications. All the instances of classes that live in a Java application are stored in the Java memory. This is also true for primitive values. What about constants? Also stored in the Java memory! And what about the method codes, native methods, field data, method data, and the order in which methods are being executed? You can probably guess that they are all stored in Java memory!

One of the tasks of the JVM is managing the Java memory. Without this memory management, no memory could be allocated and objects couldn't be stored. Even if that part was in place, it would never be cleaned up. So, cleaning up the memory, which is also called the *deallocation of objects*, is of great importance for running Java code. Without it, the code can't run, or if it's only allocated, it will get full and the program will run out of memory. How exactly this works is something will learn in *Chapter 4* when we discuss the deallocation process – called *garbage collection*.

Long story short: memory management is important. It is one of the very important tasks of the JVM. Actually, nowadays, we sort of take automatic memory management for granted, but in its early days, this was very new and special. Let's have a look at what could happen if the JVM was not managing the memory for us.

Memory management before Java

In older languages, such as C and C++, memory management was the responsibility of the developer. This meant that allocation and deallocation of a memory area had to be done using a command. For example, in C, the following code snippet shows how you could allocate some memory and assign a value to it. Please note that this is just a small example to illustrate how awesome automatic garbage collection is and in no way a complete guide to how to do memory allocation in C – there's a lot more to it:

```
int* x;
x = (int*)malloc(4 * sizeof(int));
```

int* means that x holds the value of the pointer to the base address of the memory block.

malloc, which stands for memory allocation, is a function that is used to allocate a block of memory with a specified size. In this case, that specified size is four times the size of int. The function returns the base address.

If we would then like to assign a value to the memory allocation, we need to do this by using *x – otherwise, we will be overriding the location:

```
*x = 5;
printf("Our value: %d\n", *x);
```

The preceding code snippet assigns a value of 5 to the memory location that x is pointing to. So, if we then go ahead and print the value stored in that location (*x), we will see the value of 5. It's just x, not *x, that is the memory location.

When we no longer need *x to hold the memory location, we need to manually free the memory. If we don't do this, the memory is going to be unavailable and used up unnecessarily. Here's how we could free the memory:

```
free(x);
x = NULL;
```

We use the free function to make the memory available again so that it can be reallocated later when we request another block of memory. Are we done then? No, we're not. We are still holding the pointer to that memory location. Since the memory location is freed up right now, it could be overwritten with something else and we wouldn't know what was stored at that point. Therefore, we set our pointer to NULL.

So, what would x be pointing at after freeing up the memory? Well, the very same address – but what is in there? That's uncertain. Depending on how the freeing works, it could either be empty or the old value if it's not overwritten yet, but when it's overwritten, it would be whatever it was overwritten with. In other words: a big surprise! Of course, I usually love surprises, but typically not so much when it comes to the value of the variables in my code.

Here are some common problems with doing memory management manually:

- **Dangling pointers**: This is what happens if you don't set the variable holding the pointer to NULL after freeing up the memory address.

- **Memory leaks**: This is what happens if you don't free up memory that is no longer needed. It doesn't become available again and it remains blocked unnecessarily. Eventually, you can run out of memory by holding all the values you don't need.

- **Boilerplate code**: You have a lot of code in the code base that deals with allocation and deallocation, but not so much with your business logic. All this code needs to be maintained.

- **Error-prone**: Even though developers are (usually) aware of what needs to happen, it's easy to make a small mistake and forget to free up the memory or set a pointer to NULL, for example.

There are other common pitfalls, but I believe that this is more than enough to appreciate the JVM and its garbage collector and automatic allocation. Let's see what is implemented in the JVM to be able to do all this.

Understanding the JVM's components for memory management

To be able to execute applications, the JVM has roughly three components in place. One is used to load all the classes, the **class loader**. This is actually a complex process in itself; the classes are loaded and the bytecode is verified. The loading of the classes and the execution of the bytecode requires memory. This memory is needed for storing the class data, memory allocation, and the instructions that are being executed. This is what the **runtime data areas** component is for. This is the part that this book is all about: the Java memory. When the classes are loaded, the files need to be executed. The component that executes the bytecode after it's loaded in the main memory using the first two components is commonly referred to as the **execution engine**. The execution engine interacts with the **Java Native Interface** (**JNI**) to use the native libraries that are required for executing the bytecode. These processes and the steps between them are depicted in *Figure 1.3*:

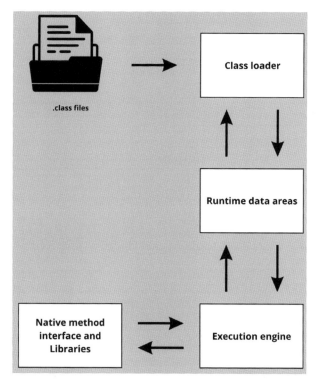

Figure 1.3 – Overview of the JVM components for application execution

Now that we know what elements the memory roughly consists of, let's explore the most important component for memory management in more detail: the runtime data area.

Runtime data area

Here are the runtime data areas of the JVM:

- The stack
- The heap
- The method area/Metaspace
- The runtime constant pool
- The program counter register
- The native method stack

The different parts of the Java memory are depicted in *Figure 1.4*:

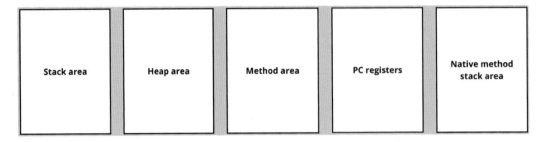

Figure 1.4 – Overview of the different runtime areas

The memory consists of different parts as shown in the picture. All these parts are needed for the Java application to run. Let us take a detailed look at each of these memory parts.

The heap

When the JVM starts, it reserves a piece of the RAM for the Java application to use for dynamic memory allocation. This memory is called the heap. This is the area where the runtime data is stored. Class instances can be found on the heap. The JVM takes care of assigning space to the heap and cleaning it up with a process called garbage collection. Assigning space is also called allocation and freeing up this space again is also called deallocation. The deallocation of objects on the heap is handled by the garbage collection process of the JVM. The garbage collection works with different areas of the heap. These different areas and garbage collection are very interesting topics and we'll discuss them in much more detail in *Chapter 3* and *Chapter 4*.

The stack

The stack, or more precisely, the JVM stack, is where the primitives and pointers to the heap are stored. For every method that is called, a frame gets created on a stack and this frame also holds the values for this method, such as partial results and return values.

There is not just one stack. Every thread in the application has its own thread. This is displayed in *Figure 1.5*:

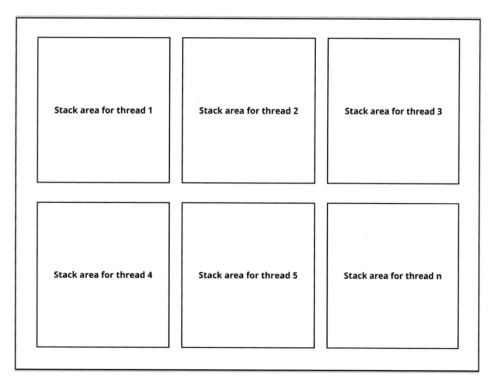

Figure 1.5 – Stack area containing stacks for every thread

A thread is a path of execution. When an application has multiple threads, this means that multiple things are happening at the same time. This happening at the same time in an application is a very important concept called **concurrency**.

This means that the stack area of the memory actually contains a lot of stacks – one for every thread. The threads can only access their own stacks and the stacks cannot have links between them.

So, the stack stores the values necessary for method execution and every thread has its own stack. The next part of the runtime data area that we're going to look at is the method area.

The method area (Metaspace)

The method area is where the runtime representation of classes is stored. The method area contains the runtime code, static variables, constants pools, and constructor code. To summarize: this is where the class's metadata is stored. All threads share this method area. The JVM only specifies the method area, but the implementation we have been dealing with since **Java 8** is called the Metaspace. The old name for this area was the **PermGen** (as in, **permanent generation**) space. There are actually also some differences between PermGen and the Metaspace, but these juicy details are for later. Don't we all love a good cliffhanger?

The PC register

The **Program Counter (PC)** register knows what code is being executed by holding the address of the instruction that is being executed in its thread. In *Figure 1.6*, you can see a depiction of this:

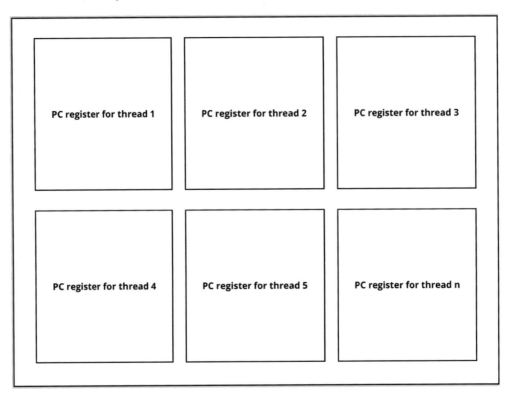

Figure 1.6 – A PC register containing a register for every thread

Every thread has its own PC register, sometimes also referred to as the call stack. It knows the sequence of statements that needs to be executed and which one it is executing currently. This is why we need a separate one for every thread – with just one PC register, we couldn't execute multiple threads at the same time!

This is similar to the stack area, as you can see when you compare *Figure 1.5* and *Figure 1.6*.

The native method stack

There's also a native method stack, also known as a **C stack**. It is there for the native code that is executed. Native code is part of the implementation that is not written in Java, but for example, in C. These are the stacks that store the values for the native code, just as the JVM stack does for the Java code. Again, every thread has its own. How these are implemented depends on the specific implementation of the

JVM. Some JVMs don't support native code; clearly, they don't need native stacks either. This can be found in the documentation of the JVM that you are using.

With this, we have seen the different parts of the Java runtime data area in a bit more detail. Chances are that a lot of new information has been thrown at you at this point, and this can be tough! Before we continue, let me explain why we even want to know this.

At this point, you might be wondering what I'm still waiting for and be itching to get started – and you're right! We'll be discussing the basics of memory management, stack and heap memory, and the Metaspace in more detail in this chapter, but first, we need to have a look at creating variables in Java.

Creating variables in Java

Creating variables in Java means that we have to declare a variable. If we also want to use it, we have to initialize it. As you most likely know, declaration is the process of assigning a type and a name. Initializing is about giving the variable an actual value:

```
int number = 3;
char letter = 'z';
```

Here, we declare the variable and initialize it on the same line. We declare it with the type and name. The types here are `int` and `char` and the variable names are `number` and `letter`. This can also be separated over multiple lines as follows:

```
double percentage;
percentage = 8.6;
```

The JVM doesn't check the types anymore – this is done by the compiler prior to running the application. There is actually a difference between the storage of primitive types and reference types. This is what we're going to look at now.

Primitives and reference types

The JVM deals with two types of variables: primitives and reference types. There are eight primitive types in Java:

- `int`
- `byte`
- `short`
- `long`
- `float`

- `double`
- `boolean`
- `char`

The primitive types store just the value, and they are limited to eight types. There are also reference types. Reference types are instances of classes. You can create your own classes. Therefore, there's no real limit to how many reference types there are.

When you create variables, there can be two types of values stored in them: primitive values and reference values. The primitive values have the type of one of the primitives. The reference value is holding a pointer to an object location.

References come in four flavors:

- Class references
- Array references
- Interface references
- `null`

Class reference types hold the (dynamically) created class objects. The array reference type has a component type. This is the type of the array. If the component type is not of the array type, it is called the element type. The array reference always has a single dimension, but the component type can be another array, creating multi-dimensional arrays. It doesn't matter how many dimensions the array has; the last component type is not of the array type and is therefore the element type. This element type can be one of three types: primitive, class, or interface.

`null` is the special case where the reference is not pointing to anything. The value of the reference is then `null`.

How are these variables stored? Primitive and reference variables are stored on the stack. The actual object is stored on the heap. Let's first have a look at storing variables on the stack.

Storing variables on the stack

Variables used in a method are stored on the stack. The stack memory is the memory that is used for executing methods. In *Figure 1.7*, we have shown a stack area for three threads, each containing several frames.

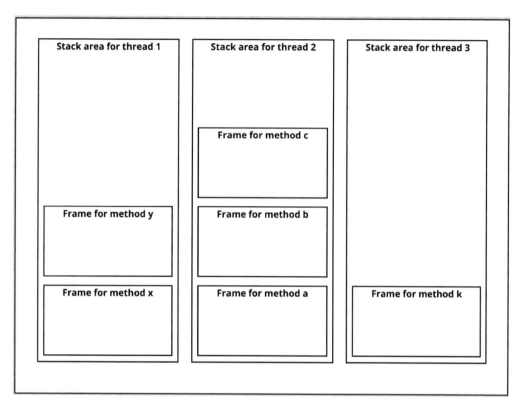

Figure 1.7 – Overview of the frames in the stack area for three threads

Inside a method, primitives and references exist. Every thread in the application has its own stack. The stack consists of frames. Every method that gets invoked comes with a new frame on the stack. When the method execution is finished, the frame is removed.

If the stack memory is too small to store what is needed for the frame, StackOverFlowError is thrown. When there is not enough space for a new stack for a new thread, OutOfMemoryError is thrown. The method that currently is being executed by a thread is called the current method and its data is held in the current frame.

Current frame and current method

The reason that a stack is named as such is that it can only access the top frame of the stack. You can compare this to a stack of plates where you can only (safely) take plates from the top. The top frame is called the current frame as it belongs to the current method – the method that is being executed at that time.

If a method that is being executed calls another method, a frame gets placed on top of the frame. This new frame becomes the current frame since the newly invoked method is the current method that is being executed.

In *Figure 1.7*, there are three current frames, because there are three threads. The current frames are the ones on top. So, let's see the following:

- The **Frame for method y** is for **thread 1**
- The **Frame for method c** is for **thread 2**
- The **Frame for method k** is for **thread 3**

When the method is executed, it gets removed. The previous frame then becomes the current frame again since the method that has called the other method is the one that gets the control back for the moment and is the method that is being executed at that time (the current method).

Elements of the frame

A frame contains a number of elements. These elements are needed to store all the necessary data for a method to be executed. An overview of all the elements can be seen in *Figure 1.8*:

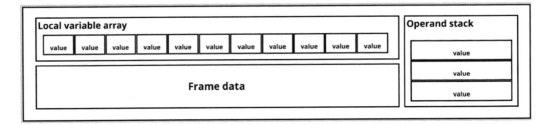

Figure 1.8 – Schematic overview of a stack frame

As you can see, a frame has a local variable array, an operand stack, and frame data. Let us explore the separate elements of the frame in more detail.

The array of local variables

The local variables of the frame are stored in an array. This array length is set during compile time. The array has single and double spots. Single spots are for types of int, short, char, float, byte, boolean, and reference. The double spots are for long and double (they are 64 bits in size).

The local variables can be accessed by their index. There are two types of methods: static methods (class methods) and instance methods. For these instance methods, the first element of the local variable array is always the reference to the object that they exist on, also known as this. Parameters that are given to the method start from index 1 on the local variable array.

For `static` methods, no instance needs to be provided to the frame, so they start with the parameters that were used to invoke them at index `0`.

The operand stack

This concept can be a bit rough, so bear with me. Every stack frame has an operand stack – a stack (operand stack) on the element (frame) of the stack – and this operand stack is used to write operands so that they can be, well, operated upon. This is where all the values fly around.

It begs for an example, so let's have a look at one. When the frame is newly created, there is nothing on the operand stack, but let's assume that the method for which the frame was created is going to do a basic mathematical operation, such as adding x and y.

x and y are local variables and their values are in the aforementioned array of local variables. In order to do the operation, their values need to be pushed to the operand stack – so, the value of x is going to be pushed first and the value of y is going to be pushed second.

The operand stack is a stack, so when it needs to access the variables, it can only grab them from the top of the stack. It pops y first and then pops x. After this, the operand stack is empty again. The operation that is being performed knows the order of the popped variables. When the operation is done, the result is pushed to the operand stack and it can be popped from there.

The operand stack is also used for other important operations, such as preparing parameters that need to be sent to a method as input and receiving the results that the methods return.

Frame data

The frame data consists of diverse data needed to execute the method. Some examples are a reference to the constant pool, how to normally return a method, and abruptly completed methods (or exceptions).

The first of these, a reference to the constant pool, requires special attention. A class file has all the symbolic references that need to be resolved in the runtime constant pool. This pool contains all the constants needed for running the class and it is generated by the compiler. It contains the names of identifiers in the class and the JVM uses this file during runtime to link the class to other classes.

Every frame has a reference to the constant pool of the current method at runtime. Since this is a runtime constant pool with symbolic references, linking needs to happen dynamically.

Let's have a look at what the constant pool looks like for our silly `Example` class. Here is the code for our `Example` class:

```
package chapter1;

public class Example {
    public static void main(String[] args) {
```

```
        int number = 3;
        char letter = 'z';
        double percentage;
        percentage = 8.6;
    }
}
```

By running the following command (after we compiled it with `javac Example.java`), we can see the constant pool:

```
javap -v Example.class
```

Here, you can see the output:

```
Classfile /Users/maaikevanputten/Documents/packt/
memorymanagement/src/main/java/chapter1/Example.class
  Last modified 12 Jun 2022; size 298 bytes
  SHA-256 checksum
b2a6321e598c50c5d97ba053ca0faf689197df18c5141b727603
eaec0fecac3e
  Compiled from "Example.java"
public class chapter1.Example
  minor version: 0
  major version: 61
  flags: (0x0021) ACC_PUBLIC, ACC_SUPER
  this_class: #9                          // chapter1/Example
  super_class: #2                         // java/lang/Object
  interfaces: 0, fields: 0, methods: 2, attributes: 1
Constant pool:
   #1 = Methodref          #2.#3          // java/lang/
Object."<init>":()V
   #2 = Class              #4             // java/lang/Object
   #3 = NameAndType        #5:#6          // "<init>":()V
   #4 = Utf8               java/lang/Object
   #5 = Utf8               <init>
   #6 = Utf8               ()V
   #7 = Double             8.6d
   #9 = Class              #10            // chapter1/Example
  #10 = Utf8               chapter1/Example
```

```
  #11 = Utf8               Code
  #12 = Utf8               LineNumberTable
  #13 = Utf8               main
  #14 = Utf8               ([Ljava/lang/String;)V
  #15 = Utf8               SourceFile
  #16 = Utf8               Example.java
{
  public chapter1.Example();
    descriptor: ()V
    flags: (0x0001) ACC_PUBLIC
    Code:
      stack=1, locals=1, args_size=1
        0: aload_0
        1: invokespecial #1                    // Method java/
lang/Object."<init>":()V
        4: return
      LineNumberTable:
        line 3: 0

  public static void main(java.lang.String[]);
    descriptor: ([Ljava/lang/String;)V
    flags: (0x0009) ACC_PUBLIC, ACC_STATIC
    Code:
      stack=2, locals=5, args_size=1
        0: iconst_3
        1: istore_1
        2: bipush        122
        4: istore_2
        5: ldc2_w        #7                     // double 8.6d
        8: dstore_3
        9: return
      LineNumberTable:
        line 5: 0
        line 6: 2
        line 8: 5
        line 9: 9
```

```
}
    SourceFile: "Example.java"
```

As you can see, the constant pool has 16 entries. These are the ones created by us, but also some created by Java. They are needed to execute the program, so the name of the program, method, and so on are created in the constant pool to run the program.

Values on the stack

The values of the primitive's local variables are stored directly in the stack – to be more precise, on the array of the frame of the method that the local variables are in. Objects are not stored on the stack. Instead, the object reference is stored on the stack. The object reference is the address at which to find the object on the heap.

Primitives and wrapper classes

Be careful not to confuse the primitive types with their object wrapper classes. They are easily recognized by the type being in uppercase. The wrapper class objects don't live on the stack, simply because they are objects. Whenever a method has been executed, the values of the associated primitives are cleaned up from the stack and they are gone forever.

Some wrapper classes are more easily recognized than others. Let's take a look at a code snippet:

```
int primitiveInt = 2;
Integer wrapperInt = 2;
char primitiveChar = 'A';
Character wrapperChar = 'A';
```

As you can see, the wrappers start with a capital and are longer. For many types, however, the word is exactly the same and the only difference is that it starts with a capital. Personally, I'm most often fooled by `Boolean` and `boolean` (I blame C# for this since the equivalent of the Java `boolean` primitive in C# is `bool`).

Here, you can see the difference between the other primitives and their reference types:

```
short primitiveShort = 15;
Short wrapperShort = 15;
long primitiveLong = 8L;
Long wrapperLong = 8L;
double primitiveDouble = 3.4;
Double wrapperDouble = 3.4;
float primitiveFloat = 5.6f;
```

```
Float wrapperFloat = 5.6f;
boolean primitiveBoolean = true;
Boolean wrapperBoolean = true;
byte primitiveByte = 0;
Byte wrapperByte = 0;
```

Please note that they have the exact same name. We need to look at the first letter to distinguish between the wrapper class and the primitive type. Wrapper classes are objects and these are created differently. Let's find out how.

Creating objects in Java

Objects are a bundle of values. In Java, they can be created by instantiating classes using the new keyword.

Here is a very basic Person class:

```java
public class Person {
    private String name;
    private String hobby;

    public String getName() {
        return name;
    }

    public void setName(String name) {
        this.name = name;
    }

    public String getHobby() {
        return hobby;
    }

    public void setHobby(String hobby) {
        this.hobby = hobby;
    }
}
```

If we want to instantiate it, we'll use the following:

```
Person p = new Person();
```

What this does is create a new `Person` object and store it on the heap. Storing on the heap deserves a bit more of an explanation. This is what we're going to zoom in on now!

Storing objects on the heap

Storing objects on the heap is very different from storing values on the stack. As we've just seen, references to places on the heap are stored on the stack. These references are memory addresses and these memory addresses translate to a certain place on the heap where the object is being stored. Without this object reference, we would have no way to access an object on the heap.

Object references have a certain type. There are very many built-in types in Java that we can use, such as `ArrayList`, `String`, all the wrapper classes, and more, but we can also create our own objects and these objects will be stored on the heap too.

The heap memory holds all the objects that exist in the application. Objects on the heap can be accessed from everywhere in the application using the address of the object, the object reference. The objects contain the same things as the blocks on the stack: the primitive values directly and the addresses for other objects on the heap.

In *Figure 1.9*, you can see an overview of the stack and the heap and what this would look like (in a simplified view) for the following Java code:

```java
public static void main(String[] args) {
    int x = 5;
    Person p = new Person();
    p.setName("maaike");
    p.setHobby("coding");
}
```

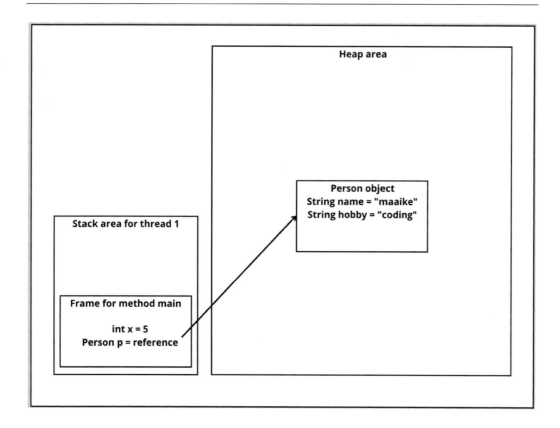

Figure 1.9 – Overview of the connection between the stack and the heap

It's very much simplified – for example, the `String` objects in the `Person` object would be separate objects themselves. We'll focus on the heap in *Chapter 3* to get a more accurate understanding of the heap area.

So, what happens when we run out of heap memory? If the application needs more heap space than is available, `OutOfMemoryError` is thrown.

Alright, we have seen the stack and the heap. There is just one memory area that we need to discuss here and that is the Metaspace.

Exploring the Metaspace

The Metaspace is the memory space that holds the class `metadata` that is necessary for runtime. It is the method area in the JVM specification and in most popular Java implementations after Java SE 7, this area is called the Metaspace.

If you know about PermGen, or you come across it, just know that this is the old memory area where all class `metadata` was stored. It had some limitations and has been replaced by the Metaspace.

So, back to this class `metadata`. What even is that? Class `metadata` is the runtime representation of the Java classes that are necessary to run the program. It actually contains a lot of things, such as the following:

- The *Klass* structure (we'll see more in *Chapter 5* when we take a deep dive into the Metaspace!)
- Bytecode of methods
- The constant pool
- Annotations and more

That's it! These are the basics of Java memory management. There is a lot more to say about the specific parts. We are going to start with a closer look at primitives and objects on the heap in the next chapter, but first, let's recap what we've done.

Summary

In this chapter, we have gone through an overview of Java memory. We started with computer memory and learned that the computer has main memory and secondary storage. The main memory is most important for us since this is what is used to run programs, including Java programs.

The main memory consists of RAM and ROM. Java applications use RAM to run. Java applications are executed by the JVM. This JVM executes Java applications and in order to do so, it has three components: a class loader, runtime data areas, and an execution engine.

We focused on the different components of the runtime data area: the heap, stack, method area, PC register, and native method stack.

The stack is the memory area that is used to store variables and values of methods in frames. The heap is used for storing objects. The stack holds references to objects on the heap. The heap is accessible from everywhere within the application and whoever has an object's address on the heap can access the object. The stack is only accessible for the thread that has created this stack.

The Metaspace is the memory area where the class metadata that is needed during runtime is stored.

In the next chapter, we're going to visualize and have a closer look at how heap and stack memory are combined.

2
Primitives and Objects in Java Memory

In *Chapter 1*, we saw the differences between primitives, objects, and references. We learned that primitives are types that come with the Java language; in other words, we do not have to define primitive types, we just use them. For example, `int x;` defines (creates) a primitive variable, `x`, which is of (the primitive) type `int`. This means that `x` can store whole integer numbers only, for example, -5, 0, 12, and so on.

We also learned that objects are instantiations of a **class** and that we use the `new` keyword to create instances of objects. For example, assuming a `Person` class exists, `new Person();` instantiates (creates) an object of type `Person`. This object will be stored on the heap.

We saw that references enable us to manipulate objects and that references are of four different types: `class`, `array`, `interface`, and `null`. When you create an object, the reference to the object is what you receive back. For example, in the code `Person p = new Person();`, the reference is `p` and it is of type `Person`. Whether the reference is placed on the stack or on the heap depends on the context – more on this later.

Understanding the differences between references and objects is very important and greatly simplifies core **object-oriented programming (OOP)** concepts, such as **inheritance** and **polymorphism**. This also helps in fixing `ClassCastException` errors. Being aware of Java's call-by-value mechanism and, in particular, how it relates to references can prevent subtle encapsulation issues known as *escaping references*.

In this chapter, we will delve more deeply into the following topics:

- Understanding primitives on the stack and heap
- Storing objects on the heap
- Managing object references and security

Technical requirements

The code for this chapter can be found on GitHub at `https://github.com/PacktPublishing/` `B18762_Java-Memory-Management`.

Understanding primitives on the stack and heap

Java comes with a predefined set of primitive data types. Primitive data types are always in lowercase, for example, `double`. Contrast primitives with their associated wrapper counterparts, which are classes in the API, have methods (primitives do not), and wrappers start with a capital letter, for example, `Double`.

The primitive data types can be broken down into integral types (whole numbers), namely `byte`, `short`, `int`, `long`, and `char`, and floating-point types (decimal numbers), namely `float`, `double`, and `boolean` (`true` or `false`).

Primitives can be stored on both the stack and the heap. They are stored on the stack when they are local variables to methods, in other words, parameters to the method or variables declared inside the method itself. Primitives are stored on the heap when they are members of a class, that is, instance variables. Instance variables are declared within the class scope, in other words, outside all of the methods. Therefore, primitive variables declared within a method go on the stack, whereas instance variables go on the heap (inside the object).

Now that we understand where primitives are stored, let us turn our attention to storing objects.

Storing objects on the heap

In this section, we are going to examine storing objects on the heap. Gaining a full understanding of this area requires a discussion comparing references and objects. We will examine their types, where they are stored, and crucially, their differences. A sample piece of code with an associated diagram will finish the section.

References

References refer to objects and enable us to access them. If we are accessing an object instance member, then we use the reference. If we are accessing a static (class) member, we use the class name.

References can be stored on both the stack and the heap. If the reference is a local variable in a method, then the reference is stored on the stack (in the local method array for that method frame). If the reference is an instance variable, then the reference is stored inside the object, on the heap.

By way of comparison with objects, we can have a reference of an **abstract class** but not an object of an abstract class. The same applies to interfaces – we can have an **interface** reference type, but you cannot instantiate an interface; that is, you cannot create an object of an interface type. Both situations are demonstrated in *Figure 2.1*:

```
 2 interface Walkable{}
 3
 4 abstract class Human{}
 5
 6 class Person extends Human implements Walkable{}
 7
 8 public class StackAndHeap {
 9⊖     public static void main(String[] args) {
10         Human h;
11         h = new Human();
12
13         Walkable w;
14         w = new Walkable();
15     }
16 }
```

Figure 2.1 – Object instantiation errors

In *Figure 2.1*, the references declared on lines 10 and 13, an abstract class and an interface reference, respectively, have no issue. However, attempting to create an object of these types on lines 11 and 14 causes errors. Feel free to try out this code, contained in ch2 folder here: https://github.com/PacktPublishing/B18762_Java-Memory-Management/tree/main/ch2. The reason for the compiler errors is that you cannot create an object based on an abstract class or interface. We will address these errors in the next section.

Now that we have discussed references, let us examine objects.

Objects

All objects are stored on the heap. To understand objects, we must first understand a fundamental construct in OOP, the class. A class is similar to the plan of a house. With the plan of the house, you can view it and discuss it, but you cannot open any doors, put the kettle on, and so on. This is what classes are in OOP – they are views of what the object will look like in memory. When the house is built, you can now open the doors, have a cup of tea, and so forth. When the object is built, you have an in-memory representation of the class. Using the reference, we can access the instance members using the dot notation syntax.

Let us address the compiler issues from *Figure 2.1* and, in addition, show the dot notation syntax in operation:

```
 2 interface Walkable{}
 3
 4 abstract class Human{}
 5
 6 class Person extends Human implements Walkable{}
 7
 8 public class StackAndHeap {
 9⊝     public static void main(String[] args) {
10         Human h;
11         h = new Person();
12         System.out.println(h.toString());
13
14         Walkable w;
15         w = new Person();
16         System.out.println(w.toString());
17     }
18 }
```

Figure 2.2 – The interface and abstract class references fixed

In *Figure 2.2*, as lines 11 and 15 compile without any error, they demonstrate that the class must be a non-abstract (concrete) class before an object based on it can be instantiated (created). Lines 12 and 16 demonstrate the dot notation syntax.

Let us now examine in more detail the creation of an object.

How to create objects

Objects are instantiated (created) using the new keyword. The purpose of new is to create an object on the heap and return its address, which we store in a reference variable. Line 11 from *Figure 2.2* has the following line of code:

```
h = new Person();
```

The reference is on the left-hand side of the assignment operator – we are initializing an h reference of type Human.

The object to be instantiated is on the right-hand side of the assignment operator – we are creating an object of type Person, and the default Person constructor is executed. This default constructor is synthesized by the compiler (as there is no explicit Person constructor present in the code).

Now that we have looked at both objects and references, let us expand the example and, using a diagram, view both the stack and heap representations.

Understanding the differences between references and objects

In order to contrast the stack and the heap, both the `Person` class and the `main()` method have been changed:

```java
 2 interface Walkable{}
 3
 4 abstract class Human{}
 5
 6 class Person extends Human implements Walkable{
 7      private String name;
 8      private int age;
 9
10⊖     Person(String aName, int aAge){
11          name = aName;
12          age  = aAge;
13      }
14⊖     @Override
15      public String toString(){
16          String decoratedName = "My name is "+name +
17                  " and I am "+ age + " years old.";
18          return decoratedName;
19      }
20 }
21
22 public class StackAndHeap {
23⊖     public static void main(String[] args) {
24          int x=0;
25          Person joeBloggs = new Person("Joe Bloggs", 23);
26          System.out.println(x);
27          System.out.println(joeBloggs.toString());
28      }
29 }
```

Figure 2.3 – Stack and heap code

Figure 2.3 details a `Person` class containing two instance variables, a constructor taking two parameters, and the `toString()` instance method. The second class, `StackAndHeap`, is the driver class (it contains the `main()` method). In `main()`, we initialize a local primitive variable, `x`, and instantiate an instance of `Person`.

Figure 2.4 shows the stack and heap representations after line 27 has been executed:

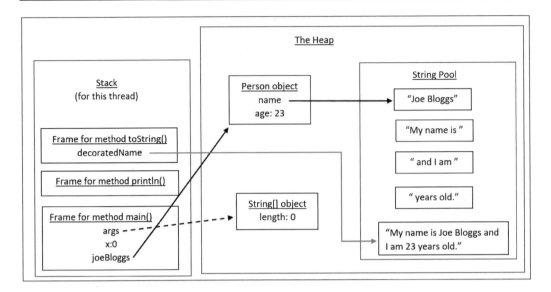

Figure 2.4 – A stack and heap representation of the code in Figure 2.3

Referring to *Figure 2.3*, the first method to execute is main() on line 23. This results in a frame for main() being pushed onto the stack. The local variables args and x are stored in the local variable array in this frame. On line 25, we create an instance of Person passing in the String literal, Joe Bloggs, and the integer literal, 23. Any String literal is itself a String object and is stored on the heap. In addition, as it is a String literal, this String object is stored in a special area of the heap called the **String Pool** (also known as the String Constant Pool).

The instance variable name inside the Person object resides on the heap and is a String type; that is, it is a reference variable, and it refers to the **Joe Bloggs** object in the String pool. The other instance variable in Person, namely age, is a primitive, and its value of 23 is stored directly inside the object on the heap. However, the reference to the Person object, joeBloggs, is stored on the stack, in the frame for the main() method.

On line 26 in *Figure 2.3*, we output the local variable, x, which outputs 0 to the standard output device (typically the screen). Line 27 is then executed, as shown in *Figure 2.4*. First, the println() method from PrintStream (out is of type PrintStream) causes a frame to be pushed onto the stack. In order to simplify the diagram, we have not gone into any detail in that stack frame. Before println() can complete execution, joeBloggs.toString() must first be executed.

As the toString() method in Person has now been invoked/called, a new frame for toString() is pushed onto the stack on top of the println() frame. Next, toString() builds up a local String variable named decoratedName using String literals and the instance variables.

As you are probably aware, if you have a `String` instance on the left or the right of a + operator, the overall operation becomes a `String` append and you end up with a `String` result.

These `String` literals are stored in the String Pool. The final `String` result is *My name is Joe Bloggs and I am 23 years old*, which is assigned to the local variable, `decoratedName`. This String is returned from `toString()` back to the `println()` statement on line 27 that called it. The returned `String` is then echoed to the screen.

That concludes our section on storing objects on the heap. Now we will turn our attention to areas that can cause subtle issues in your code. However, now that we have separated the reference from the object, these issues will be much easier to understand and fix.

Managing object references and security

In this section, we are going to examine object references and a subtle security issue that can arise if references are not managed with due care. This security issue is called *escaping references* and we will explain when and how it occurs with the aid of an example. In addition, we will fix the issue in the example, demonstrating how to address this security concern.

Inspecting the escaping references issue

In this section, we will discuss and provide an example of Java's call-by-value parameter passing mechanism. Once we understand call-by-value, this will enable us to demonstrate the issue that occurs when passing (or returning) references. Let us start with Java's call-by-value mechanism.

Call-by-value

Java uses call-by-value when passing parameters to methods and returning results from methods. Put simply, this means that Java *makes a copy of something*. In other words, when you are passing an argument to a method, a copy is made of that argument, and when you are returning a result from a method, a copy is made of that result. Why do we care? Well, what you are copying – a primitive or a reference – can have major implications (especially for mutable types, such as **StringBuilder** and **ArrayList**). This is what we want to dig into further here. We will use a sample program and an associated diagram to help. *Figure 2.5* shows the sample code:

```
 3 class Person{
 4       private String name;
 5       private int age;
 6
 7⊖      Person(String name, int age) {
 8            this.age = age;
 9            this.name = name;
10       }
11⊖      public String getName() {
12            return name;
13       }
14⊖      public void setName(String name) {
15            this.name = name;
16       }
17⊖      public int getAge() {
18            return age;
19       }
20⊖      public void setAge(int age) {
21            this.age = age;
22       }
23 }
24
25 public class CallByValue {
26⊖      public static void main(String[] args) {
27            int age=20;
28            Person john = new Person("John", age);
29            change(john, age);
30            System.out.println(john.getName()
31                  + " " + age); // Michael 20
32       }
33⊖      public static void change(Person adult, int age){
34            age = 90;
35            adult.setName("Michael");
36       }
37 }
```

Figure 2.5 – A call-by-value code sample

Figure 2.5 details a program where we have a simple `Person` class with two properties: a `String` name and an `int` (primitive) age. The constructor enables us to initialize the object state, and we have accessor/mutator methods for the instance variables.

The `CallByValue` class is the driver class. In `main()` on line 27, a local primitive `int` variable, namely `age`, is declared and initialized to 20. On line 28, we create an object of type `Person`, passing in the `String` literal, `John`, and the primitive variable, `age`. Based on these arguments, we initialize the object state. The reference, namely john, is the local variable used to store the reference to the Person object on the heap. *Figure 2.6* shows the state of memory after line 28 has finished executing. For clarity, we have omitted the args array object.

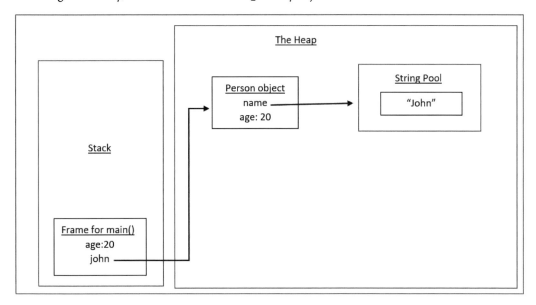

Figure 2.6 – The initial state of the stack and the heap

As *Figure 2.6* shows, the frame for the main() method is the current frame on the stack. It contains two local variables: the int primitive age with its value of 20 and the Person reference, john, referring to the Person object on the heap. The Person object has its two instance variables initialized: the age primitive variable is set to 20 and the name String instance variable is referring to the *John* String object in the String Pool (as *John* is a String literal, Java stores it there).

Now, we execute line 29, change(john, age); in *Figure 2.5*. This is where it gets interesting. We call the change() method, passing down the john reference and the age primitive. As Java is call-by-value, a copy is made of each of the arguments. *Figure 2.7* shows the stack and the heap just as we enter the change() method and are about to execute its first instruction on line 34:

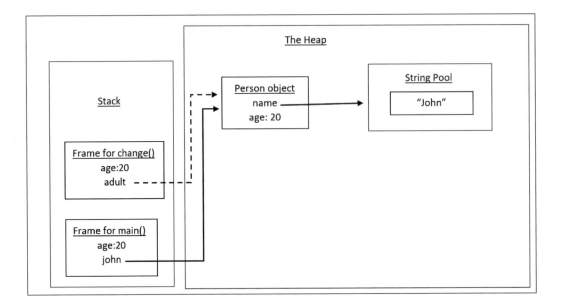

Figure 2.7 – The stack and heap as the change() method is entered

In the preceding figure, we can see that a frame has been pushed onto the stack for the change() method. As Java is call-by-value, a copy is made of both arguments into local variables in the method, namely age and adult. The difference here is crucial and requires subsections as a result.

Copying a primitive

Copying a primitive is similar to photocopying a sheet of paper. If you hand the photocopy to someone else, they can do whatever they want to that sheet – you still have the original. This is what is going to happen in this program; the called change() method will alter the primitive age variable, but the copy of age back in main() will be untouched.

Copying a reference

Copying a reference is similar to copying a remote control for a television. If you hand the second/copy remote to someone else, they can change the channel that you are watching. This is what is going to happen in this program; the called change() method will, using the adult reference, alter the name instance variable in the Person object and the john reference back in main() will see that change.

Going back to the code example from *Figure 2.5*, *Figure 2.8* shows the stack and heap after lines 34 and 35 have finished executing but *before* the change() method returns to main():

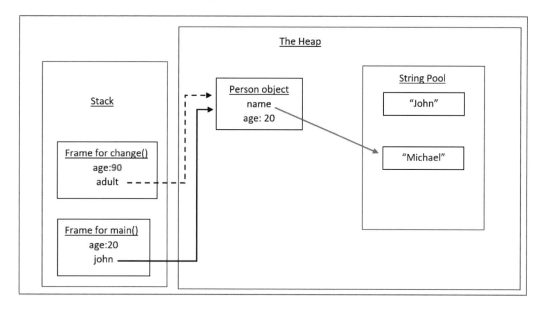

Figure 2.8 – The stack and heap as the change() method is exiting

As can be seen, the age primitive in the method frame for change() has been changed to 90. In addition, a new String literal object is created for *Michael* in the String Pool and the name instance variable in the Person object is referring to it. This is because String objects are immutable; that is, once initialized, you cannot change the contents of String objects. Note that the *John* String object in the String Pool is now eligible for garbage collection, as there are no references to it.

Figure 2.9 show the state of the stack and heap after the change() method has finished executing and control has returned to the main() method:

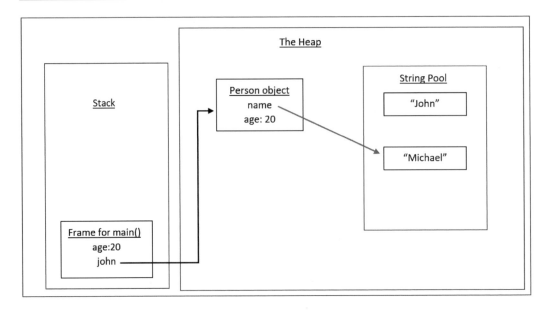

Figure 2.9 – The stack and heap after the change() method has finished

In *Figure 2.9*, the frame on the stack for the `change()` method has been popped. The frame for the `main()` method is now, once again, the current frame. You can see that the `age` primitive is unchanged, that is, it is still `20`. The reference is also the same. However, the `change()` method was able to change the instance variable that `john` was looking at. Line 30, `System.out.println(john.getName() + " " + age);`, proves what has occurred by outputting *Michael 20*.

Now that we understand Java's call-by-value mechanism, we will now discuss escaping references with the aid of an example.

The problem

The principle of encapsulation in OOP is that a class's data is `private` and accessible to external classes via its `public` API. However, in certain situations, this is not enough to protect your `private` data due to escaping references. *Figure 2.10* is an example of a class that suffers from escaping references:

```
 3 class Person {
 4      private StringBuilder name;
 5
 6⊖      Person(StringBuilder name) {
 7          this.name = name;
 8      }
 9⊖      public StringBuilder getName() {
10          return name;
11      }
12 }
13
14 public class EscapingReferences {
15⊖     public static void main(String[] args) {
16          StringBuilder sb = new StringBuilder("Dan");
17          Person p = new Person(sb);
18          sb.append("Dan");
19          System.out.println(p.getName()); // DanDan
20
21          StringBuilder sb2 = p.getName();
22          sb2.append("Dan");
23          System.out.println(p.getName()); // DanDanDan
24      }
25 }
```

Figure 2.10 – Code with escaping references

The preceding figure contains a Person class with one private instance variable, a StringBuilder called name. The Person constructor initializes the instance variable based on the argument passed in. The class also provides a public getName() accessor method to enable external classes to retrieve the private instance variable.

The driver class here is EscapingReferences. In main(), on line 16, a local StringBuilder object is created, containing the String *Dan* and sb is the name of the local reference. This reference is passed into the Person constructor in order to initialize the name instance variable in the Person object. *Figure 2.11* shows the stack and heap at this point, that is, just after line 17 has finished executing. The String Pool is omitted, in the interests of clarity.

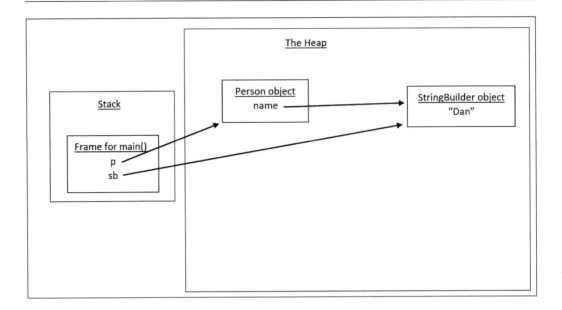

Figure 2.11 – Escaping references on the way in

At this point, the issue of escaping references is emerging. Upon executing the Person constructor, a copy of the sb reference is passed in, where it is stored in the name instance variable. Now, as *Figure 2.11* shows, both the name instance variable and the local main() variable, sb, refer to the same StringBuilder object!

Now, when line 18 executes in main(), that is, sb.append("Dan");, the object is changed to DanDan for *both* the local sb reference and the name instance variable. When we output the instance variable on line 19, it outputs *DanDan*, reflecting the change.

So, that is one issue on the way in: initializing our instance variables to the (copies of) the references passed in. We will address how to fix that shortly. On the way out, however, we also have an issue. *Figure 2.12* demonstrates this issue:

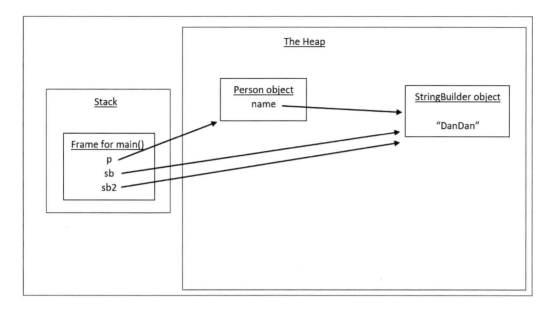

Figure 2.12 – Escaping references on the way out

Figure 2.12 shows the stack and heap after line 21, `StringBuilder sb2 = p.getName();`, executes. Again, we have a local reference, this time called `sb2`, which refers to the same object that the `name` instance variable in the `Person` object on the heap is referring to. Thus, when we use the `sb2` reference to append `Dan` to the `StringBuilder` object and then output the instance variable, we get `DanDanDan`.

At this point, it is clear that just having your data `private` is not enough. The problem arises because `StringBuilder` is a mutable type, which means, at any time, you can change the (original) object. Contrast this with `String` objects, which are immutable (as are the wrapper types, for example: `Double`, `Integer`, `Float`, and `Character`).

> **Immutability**
>
> Java protects `String` objects because any change to a `String` object results in the creation of a completely new object (with the changes reflected). Thus, the code requesting a *change* will see the requested change (it's just that it is a completely new object). The original `String` object that others may have been looking at is still untouched.

Now that we have discussed the issues with escaping references, let us examine how to solve them.

Finding a solution

Essentially, the solution revolves around a practice known as *defensive copying*. In this scenario, we do not want to store a copy of the reference for any mutable object. The same holds for returning references to our `private` mutable data in our accessor methods – we do not want to return a copy of the reference to the calling code.

Therefore, we need to be careful both on the way in and on the way out. The solution is to copy the object contents completely in both scenarios. This is known as a deep copy (whereas copying the references only is known as a shallow copy). Thus, on the way in, we copy the contents of the object into a new object and store the reference to the new object. On the way out, we copy the contents again and return the reference to the new object. We have protected our code in both scenarios. *Figure 2.13* shows the solution to the previous code from *Figure 2.10*:

```
3 class Person {
4      private StringBuilder name;
5
6⊖     Person(StringBuilder name) {
7          this.name = new StringBuilder(name.toString());
8      }
9⊖     public StringBuilder getName() {
10          return new StringBuilder(name.toString());
11      }
12 }
13
14 public class EscapingReferences {
15⊖     public static void main(String[] args) {
16          StringBuilder sb = new StringBuilder("Dan");
17          Person p = new Person(sb);
18          sb.append("Dan");
19          System.out.println(p.getName()); // Dan
20
21          StringBuilder sb2 = p.getName();
22          sb2.append("Dan");
23          System.out.println(p.getName()); // Dan
24      }
25 }
```

Figure 2.13 – Escaping references code fixed

Line 7 shows the creation of the copy object on the way in (the constructor). Line 10 shows the creation of the copy object on the way out (the accessor method). Both lines 19 and 23 output `Dan`, as they should. *Figure 2.14* represents the stack and heap as the program is about to exit:

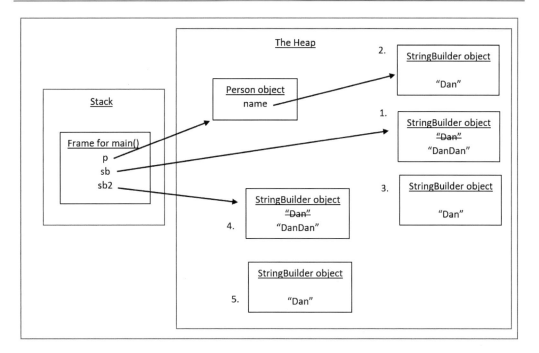

Figure 2.14 – The stack and heap for escaping references code fix

For clarity, we omit the String Pool. We have numbered the StringBuilder objects 1 to 5. We can match the objects to the code as follows:

- Line 16 creates object 1.

- Line 17, which calls line 7, creates object 2. The Person instance variable name refers to this object.

- Line 18 modifies object 1, changing it to DanDan (note, however, that the object referred to by the name instance variable, that is, object 2, is untouched).

- Line 19 creates object 3. The reference is passed back to main() but never stored. As *Dan* is output, this proves that the defensive copying on the way *in* is working.

- Line 21 creates object 4. The local main() reference, sb2, refers to it.

- Line 22 amends object 4 to *DanDan* (leaving the object that the instance variable is referring to untouched).

- Line 23 creates object 5. As *Dan* is output, this proves that the defensive copying on the way *out* is working.

Figure 2.14 shows that the StringBuilder object referred to by the name instance variable never changes from *Dan*. This is exactly what we wanted.

That wraps up this chapter. We have covered a lot, so let us recap the major points.

Summary

In this chapter, we started by examining how primitives are stored in memory. Primitives are predefined types that come with the language and can be stored on both the stack (local variables) and on the heap (instance variables). It is easy to identify primitives as they have all lowercase letters.

In contrast, objects are only stored on the heap. In discussing objects, it was necessary to distinguish between references and the objects themselves. We discovered that while references can be of any type (interface, abstract class, and class), objects themselves can only be of proper, concrete classes, meaning the class must not be **abstract**.

Manage object references with care. If not managed properly, you could end up with *escaping references*. Java uses call-by-value, which means a copy is made of the argument passed or returned. Depending on whether the argument is a primitive or reference, it can have major implications. If it's a copy of a reference to a mutable type, then the calling code can change your supposedly `private` data. This is not proper encapsulation.

We examined code with this issue and associated diagrams of the stack and heap. The solution is to use defensive copying, that is, copying the object contents both on the way in and on the way out. *Thus, the references and the objects they refer to remain private.* Lastly, we detailed the code solution and associated diagrams of the stack and heap.

In the next chapter, we are going to take a closer look at the heap, the area of memory where objects live.

3
Zooming in on the Heap Space

In *Chapter 2*, we discussed the differences between references and objects in memory. References and the objects to which they refer are closely related. We discovered that Java's call-by-value mechanism could lead to a security issue known as **escaping references**, in addition to mutable objects. With the aid of sample code and diagrams, we examined the issues and how to resolve them using defensive copying.

We know that primitives and references can live on both the stack and the heap, whereas objects just live on the heap. Now, we are ready to take a closer look at the heap in preparation for the next chapter, which is on **garbage collection** (**GC**). In this chapter, we are going to cover the following topics:

- Exploring the different generations on the heap
- Learning how the spaces are used

Exploring the different generations on the heap

The heap space consists of two different memory areas:

- Young generation space
- Old generation (tenured) space.

While we will not dive into the **GC** process in this chapter, we need to explain what a *live* object is. A live object is one that is reachable from the GC roots.

Garbage collection roots

A GC root is a special type of live object and is, therefore, not eligible for GC. All objects reachable from GC roots are also live and are, therefore, not eligible for GC. The GC roots act as starting points in GC, that is, start at these roots and mark all objects reachable as *live*. The most common GC roots are the following:

- Local variables on the stack
- All active Java threads

- Static variables (as these can be referenced by their classes)
- **Java Native Interface (JNI)** references – Objects created by the native code as part of a JNI call. This is a very special case of GC roots because the JVM does not know whether the objects are referenced by the native code or not.

Let us examine how the spaces appear in memory, as shown in *Figure 3.1*:

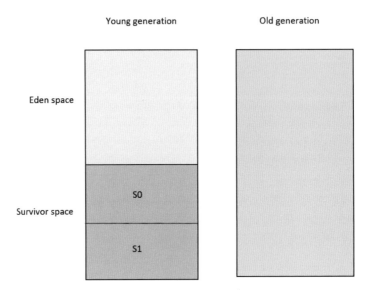

Figure 3.1 – The heap generations

At this point, we require brief definitions so that we can discuss how the spaces are used:

- **Young generation space** – The young generation space, sometimes called the **nursery** or **new** space, contains two separate areas: the **eden** space and the **survivor** space. Both serve different functions with the overall goal to increase memory efficiency. We will discuss them in turn:

  - **Eden space:** *New* objects are allocated in the eden space. When the eden space is full and there is no room for allocating a new object, the young generation (**minor**) garbage collector runs.

  - **Survivor space:** There are two equally divided survivor spaces, namely S0 and S1. The minor garbage collector uses these regions in an alternate fashion. We will explore this in more detail later.

- **Old generation space** – This is also known as **tenured** space. This is where longer-lived objects reside. In other words, the garbage collector moves objects that have survived a certain number of GCs here. When the tenured space becomes full, this triggers a **major** GC.

Now that we have a brief overview of the spaces, let us examine how they are used.

Learning how the spaces are used

To understand how these different spaces are used, we will explain them in two different stages. Initially, we will examine how the spaces are used in the minor GC algorithm. Subsequently, with the aid of an example, we will show the algorithm in action.

Understanding the minor garbage collection algorithm

Let us start with the minor GC algorithm. *Figure 3.2* is high-level pseudocode of the minor GC process:

```
- Eden space is full => minor garbage collector runs:
   - Run #1:
      - assuming we are initially using S0 as the target survivor space
      - copy live objects from eden into S0; age=1
      - examine live objects in S1:
         - is age+1 >= threshold
             Y: copy object to old generation space
             N: copy object to S0, age=age+1
      - reclaim eden and S1
      - allocate object in eden

   - Run #2:
      - this time, S1 is the target survivor space
      - copy live objects from eden into S1; age=1
      - examine live objects in S0:
         - is age+1 >= threshold
             Y: copy object to old generation space
             N: copy object to S1, age=age+1
      - reclaim eden and S0
      - allocate object in eden

 - Old generation space is full => major garbage collector runs
      - tidies up old generation space
```

Figure 3.2 – Pseudocode of the minor garbage collection algorithm

Let us examine the process outlined in the preceding figure using a *Given-When-Then* scenario.

- **Given**: **S0** as the target survivor and **S1** as the source survivor spaces initially.

- **When**: Minor garbage collector runs. In other words, the eden space does not have enough space for an object that the JVM wishes to allocate.

- **Then**:

  - All live objects from the eden space are copied to the **S0** survivor space. The ages of these objects are set to 1, as they have just survived their first GC cycle.

- **S1** is examined and any live objects whose ages meet a given threshold (the **tenuring threshold**) are copied to the old generation space, meaning they are tenured. In other words, this is a long-lived object, so copy it to the old generation area where longer-lived objects reside. This makes future minor GC runs more efficient as it ensures these same objects are not re-examined.

- The remaining live **S1** objects (the ones that were not tenured) are copied to **S0**, where their ages are incremented by one, as they have just passed another GC cycle.

Note that the tenuring threshold is configurable using a JVM argument, `-XX:MaxTenuringThreshold`. In effect, this flag allows you to customize how many GC cycles an object will stay in the survivor space before it finally gets tenured into the old space. However, care must be exercised with the argument, as a value greater than 15 specifies that objects should never tenure, thereby indefinitely filling up the survivor space with old objects.

Figure 3.3 shows the process just discussed:

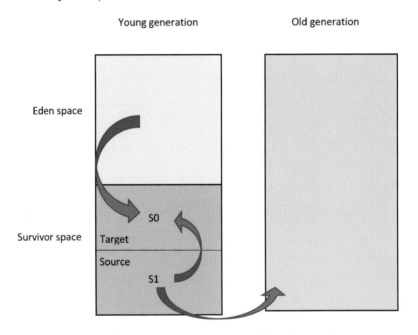

Figure 3.3 – Minor garbage collection with S0 as the target space

Here is a summary:

- Copy live eden objects to **S0** (ages set to 1)

- Copy old, live **S1** objects to long-generation space

- Copy young, live **S1** objects to **S0** (ages incremented)

Now that the live objects from eden and **S1** have been copied (saved), both eden and **S1** can now be reclaimed.

When the minor collector runs again, given that **S0** was the target survivor space the last time, **S1** will be the target survivor space this time. Therefore, all live objects from eden are copied into **S1** with ages of 1 set for each object. As **S1** is now the target space, **S0** becomes the source space. The garbage collector examines **S0** and copies long-lived objects into tenured space and short-lived objects into **S1**. *Figure 3.4* shows this process:

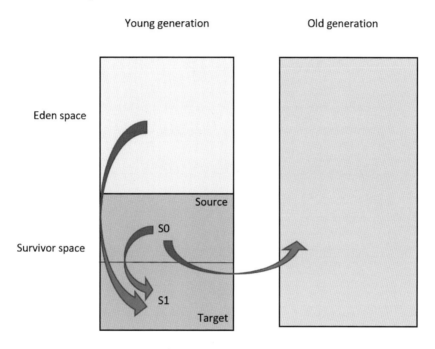

Figure 3.4 – Minor garbage collection with S1 as the target space

Here is a summary:

- All live eden objects are copied to **S1** (ages set to 1)
- Copy old, live **S0** objects to long-generation space
- Copy young, live **S0** objects to **S1** (ages incremented)

Given that the live objects from eden and **S0** have been copied, both eden and **S0** can be reclaimed.

Now that we have discussed how the spaces are used, we will enhance our explanation with the aid of an example.

Demonstrating the minor garbage collection algorithm in action

Figure 3.5 shows the situation in memory initially, prior to the first run of the minor garbage collector:

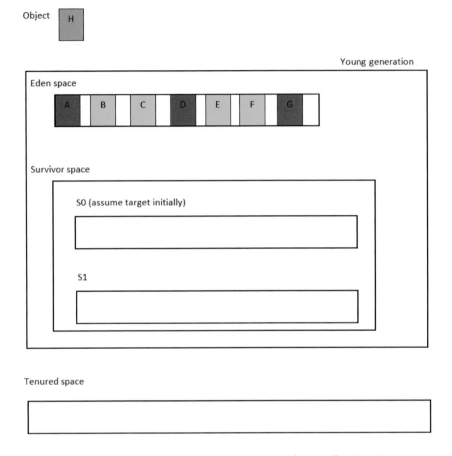

Figure 3.5 – Initial heap state prior to minor garbage collection #1

In the preceding figure, object **H** represents an object that the JVM is trying to allocate memory for in the eden space. The eden space consists of the following:

- Red objects have no references to them from the GC roots. They are eligible for GC.

- Green objects are live objects, meaning they are GC roots or can be reached via GC roots. These objects are *not* eligible for GC.

- White spaces are gaps in the eden space. If there is enough contiguous space to allocate the object, then the object is stored in eden, and its reference is returned. If, however, due to memory fragmentation, there is not enough contiguous space to allocate the object, a minor (young generation) GC is triggered.

The survivor space consists of the following:

- **S0** – Empty initially; we will assume that the JVM is using this as the target survivor space initially

- **S1** – Also empty initially; as **S0** is the target space, **S1** becomes the source space (as there is nothing in **S1** initially, this has no effect the first time around)

The tenured (old generation) space consists of long-lived objects. Long-lived objects are objects that have survived a certain predefined number of minor GC. This is a customizable threshold value using the -XX:MaxTenuringThreshold JVM argument.

As can be seen in *Figure 3.5*, the JVM has a requirement to allocate an object **H** but as there is not enough room in eden, this triggers a minor (young generation) GC. Objects **A, D,** and **G** can be removed from eden, and objects **B, C, E,** and **F** can be moved to **S0**. The eden space is reclaimed and object **H** is allocated.

Figure 3.6 shows the heap after the first minor GC has finished:

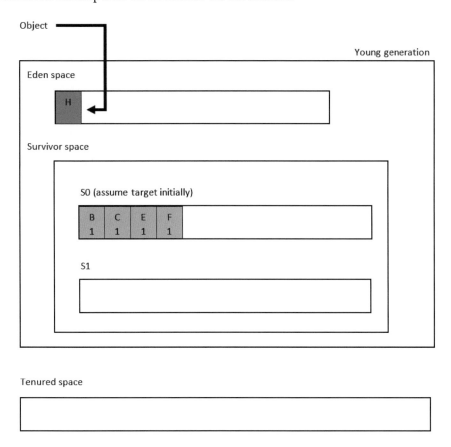

Figure 3.6 – Heap state post minor garbage collection #1

In the preceding figure, object **H** is allocated in eden, and objects **B, C, E,** and **F** in **S0**. Note that the objects in **S0** each have an age of **1** as this is their first minor GC to survive.

Figure 3.7 shows the heap prior to the second minor GC run:

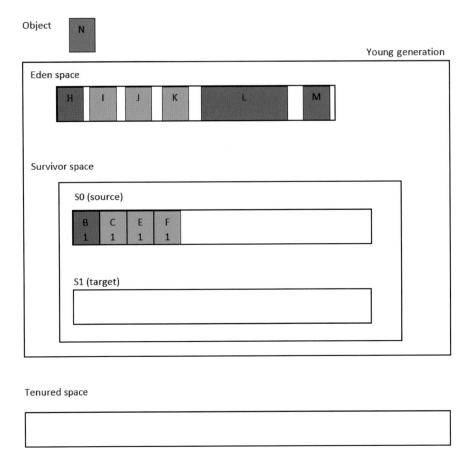

Figure 3.7 – Heap state prior to minor garbage collection #2

In *Figure 3.7*, the JVM is trying to allocate object **N** but there is no space for it in eden. This will trigger the minor garbage collector to run (for the second time). In the eden space, objects **H, L,** and **M** are eligible for GC, and objects **I, J,** and **K** are live. In the survivor space, **S0**, object **B** is now eligible for GC, whereas objects **C, E,** and **F** are live.

Figure 3.8 shows the heap after the second minor GC run:

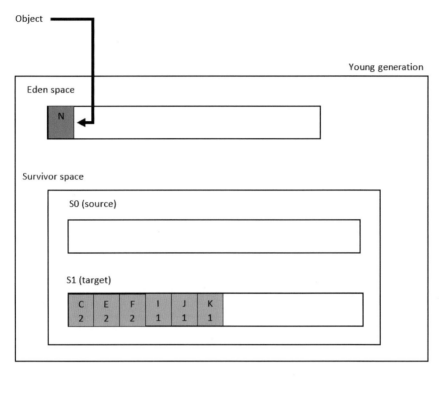

Figure 3.8 – Heap state post minor garbage collection #2

In *Figure 3.8*, **S1** is now the target survivor space and thus **S0** is the source. The garbage collector moves the live objects **C**, **E**, and **F** from **S0** to **S1**, incrementing their age values from **1** to **2**. The garbage collector then reclaims the **S0** space.

Objects **I**, **J**, and **K** are moved from eden to **S1** with age values of **1**, as this is their first time surviving a minor GC. The eden space is reclaimed and the object **N** is allocated.

The last thing to show is objects moving to the tenured space. This is what *Figure 3.9* demonstrates:

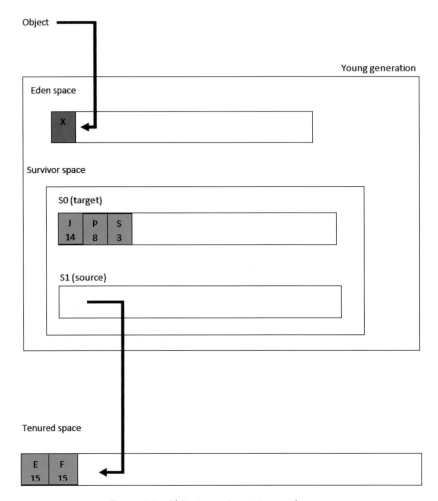

Figure 3.9 – Objects moving to tenured space

Figure 3.9 represents the heap after 15 minor GC runs. Objects **E** and **F** move to tenured space because their age values of **15** have reached the threshold (the default threshold value is 15). The next time the minor garbage collector runs, both of these objects will not feature, enabling the garbage collector to run more efficiently.

Object **X** was the object that triggered the minor garbage collector and, for this iteration, **S1** was the source and **S0** the target survivor space. Objects **J**, **P**, and **S** are still live and move from **S1** to **S0** with age counts of **14**, **8**, and **3**, respectively.

Before we conclude this chapter, it is worth mentioning some other relevant JVM flags:

- -Xms and -Xmx specify the heap's minimum and maximum sizes, respectively.

- `-XX:NewSize` and `-XX:MaxNewSize` specify the young generation's minimum and maximum sizes, respectively.

- `-XX:SurvivorRatio` specifies the relative sizes of the two survivor spaces with respect to the eden space. For example, `-XX: SurvivorRatio=6` sets the ratio between eden and a survivor space to `1:6`. In other words, each survivor space will be one-sixth the size of eden and therefore, one-eighth the size of the young generation (not one-seventh, as there two survivor spaces).

- `-XX:NewRatio` expresses the relative size of the new generation with respect to the old generation. For example, `-XX:NewRatio=3` sets the ratio between the new generation and old generation to `1:3`. This means that the new generation (eden plus both survivor spaces) occupies 25% of the heap and the old generation occupies the remaining 75%.

- `-XX:PretenureSizeThreshold` – If an object's size is greater than the size specified by this flag, then the object is tenured immediately, meaning the object is allocated straight to the old generation space. The default value is `0`, which means no object will be directly allocated to the old generation of the heap.

In general, keep the young generation space between 25% and 33% of the total heap size. This ensures that the old-generation space is always larger. This is desirable because full GCs are more expensive than minor ones.

That wraps up this chapter. Let us recap the major points.

Summary

In this chapter, we zoomed in on the heap space. We started by examining the different generations on the heap – namely, the young generation space and the old generation (tenured) space.

The young generation space is divided into two spaces: the eden and survivor spaces. The eden space is where new objects are allocated. The survivor space consists of two equally sized spaces, namely S0 and S1. The minor (young generation) garbage collector uses these survivor spaces when reclaiming memory. Minor GC is triggered when there is not enough contiguous space to allocate an object in the eden space. Using pseudocode and diagrams, we examined how the minor garbage collector utilizes the generations and spaces. We then used an example that had several use case scenarios to reinforce the concepts.

The tenured space is where longer-lived objects reside. We saw that if an object survives several GC cycles, the object moves to tenured space to make subsequent minor GC cycles more efficient. Lastly, we looked at relevant JVM flags.

Now that we understand the heap and have had a high-level overview of the minor garbage collector, we are ready to take a deep dive into GC, which is the topic of the next chapter.

4

Freeing Memory with Garbage Collection

Allocated memory needs to be deallocated when it is no longer needed. In some languages, the developer needs to take care of that. In some others, such as Java, this happens automatically. For Java, the garbage collector does this. The deallocation of memory is necessary for an application to keep running. Without the ability to free memory when it is no longer needed, we would only be able to allocate memory once, and eventually, we would run out of memory. In this chapter, we will be learning more about freeing memory on the heap using the garbage collector.

This can be a tough topic! Before you are ready for this chapter, you'll need to have a clear understanding of the heap space. Again, we'll visualize the concepts as much as possible to increase your understanding.

Here are the topics that will be discussed:

- Object eligibility for **garbage collection (GC)**
- Marking by the garbage collector
- Sweeping by the garbage collector
- Different GC implementations

Technical requirements

The code for this chapter can be found on GitHub at `https://github.com/PacktPublishing/B18762_Java-Memory Management`.

Being eligible for GC

We already know that objects on the heap are removed when they are no longer needed. The right question to ask, then, would be, *when are objects no longer needed?*

That question is easy to answer but leads to a complex problem at the same time. Let's first have a look at the answer: *objects on the heap are no longer needed when they don't have a connection to the stack.*

Objects don't have a connection to the stack when the stack doesn't store the reference to the object in a variable. Here is a simple example:

```
Object o = new Object();
System.out.println(o);
o = null;
```

In the first line, we create the object, which gets created on the heap. The o variable holds a reference to an object of type Object on the stack. We use the object because we have the reference stored. In this case, we are printing it on the second line of the example, which is clearly a rather silly output since the toString() method of Object is only going to be returning the following output to the console:

```
java.lang.Object@4617c264
```

In the next line, we set the variable to null. This overrides the reference to the object and simply points nowhere, as there is no object stored in o anymore. Nothing else in our application holds a reference to the Object we've created. Thus, it becomes eligible for GC.

This example was rather simple. To demonstrate how difficult this problem actually is, let's look at a slightly more complex problem and illustrate it with some diagrams. The question that we need to answer here is, *which objects are eligible for GC on each line?*

```
Person p1 = new Person(); // 1
Person p2 = new Person(); // 2
Person p3 = new Person(); // 3
List<Person> personList = Arrays.asList(p1, p2, p3); // 4
p1 = null; // 5
personList = null; // 6
```

This code snippet has a heap and stack that could look somewhat like *Figure 4.1* after the first four lines.

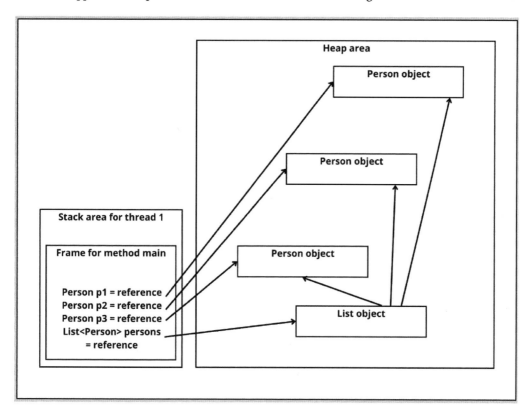

Figure 4.1 – Overview of the stack and heap for the eligibility example

On the fifth line, we set our p1 to null. Does this mean that p1 is eligible for GC? Quick reminder: an object on the heap is eligible for GC as soon as it doesn't have a connection to the stack anymore. But let's look at what happens after executing line 5:

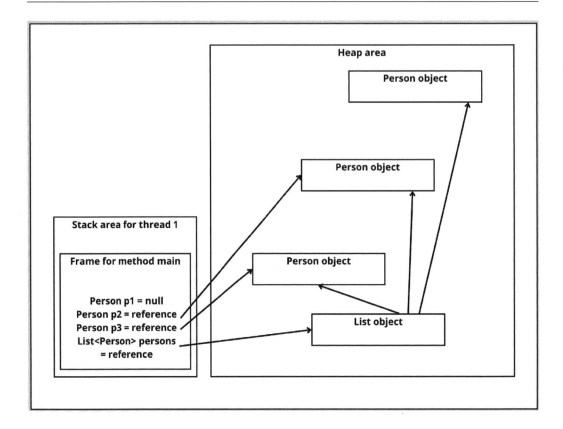

Figure 4.2 – Overview of the heap and the stack after executing line 5

As we can see, the connection to the stack in `p1` is gone. But this doesn't mean that there's no connection to the stack anymore. There's still an indirect connection. We can go from the stack to the list of `Person` object, and from there we can still access the object that `p1` was holding a reference to, since the list still holds a reference to that object. Therefore, none of the objects on the heap is eligible for GC after line 5.

This changes after line 6. At line 6, we set the variable that held the list to `null`. This means that `p1` no longer has a connection to the stack after this line, as you can see in *Figure 4.3*.

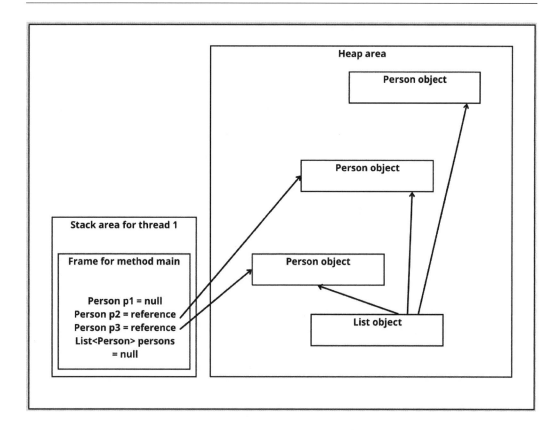

Figure 4.3 – Overview of the heap and stack at the end of the code

There is no connection between the list and the stack, and now both the List object and the first instance of the Person object are eligible for GC. Meanwhile, the p2 and p3 variables still hold a reference to the objects on the heap, and therefore these objects are not eligible for GC.

It's not hard to tell which ones are ready for GC once you understand the direct and indirect connection from the heap back to the stack. However, figuring out which ones have a connection with the stack will require some time, and this will slow down the rest of the application. There are a few ways to do it, but each comes with its own downsides with respect to accuracy or performance.

This complex problem is language-agnostic: how do we determine whether an object still has a connection to the stack? The solution we'll be discussing is of course Java-specific. Finding objects that are no longer needed is done by the garbage collector in the marking phase. The marking phase consists of a special algorithm that determines what objects are eligible for GC.

Marking by the garbage collector

Marking marks any live objects and anything not marked as ready to be garbage collected. The objects keep a special bit that determines whether they are marked or not. Upon creation, the bit is 0. In the mark phase, if an object is still in use and should not be removed, it gets set to 1.

The heap is constantly changing and so is the stack. Objects on the heap that do not have a connection to the step are eligible for GC. They are unreachable and there is no possible way for the application to be using these objects. The objects that are not ready for removal are marked; the unmarked objects will be removed.

How exactly this is implemented differs depending on the implementation of Java and the specific garbage collector you are using. But at a high level, this process starts from the stack. All the object references on the stack are followed and the objects are marked.

If we look at our previous example, this is how they would be marked. We are using the following code sample where we do not set the reference of personList to null:

```
Person p1 = new Person(); // 1
Person p2 = new Person(); // 2
Person p3 = new Person(); // 3
List<Person> personList = Arrays.asList(p1, p2, p3); // 4
p1 = null; // 5
```

Before the GC starts, all the objects are unmarked. This means the special bit is 0, which is the value they get upon creation.

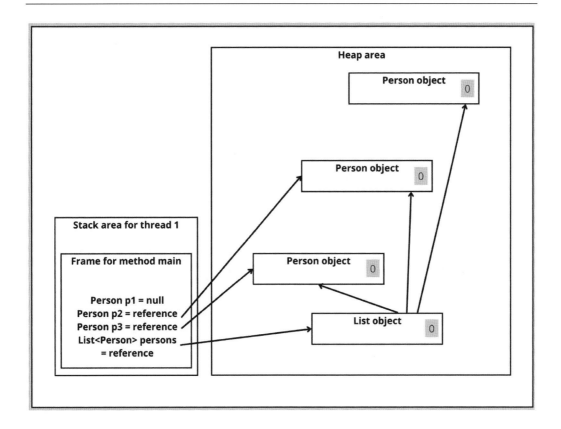

Figure 4.4 – Before garbage collection starts, none of the objects is marked

So, to start off with, all of them are unmarked, as we can tell from all the 0 after the objects. The next step is to mark the objects with a connection to the stack by changing the 0 to a 1.

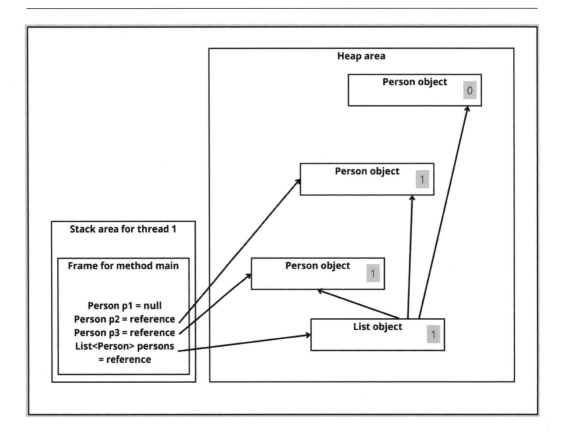

Figure 4.5 – Marking step one: direct connection to the stack

But it's not enough to just mark the ones with a direct connection to the stack. Right now, the object referred to by Person p1 would be eligible for GC even though it is reachable. This is also why the references of each object are also traveled and marked, until there are no more nested objects. *Figure 4.6* shows what our example looks like after the marking phase.

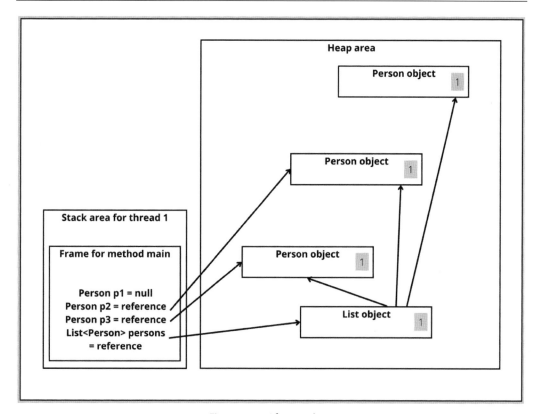

Figure 4.6 – After marking

All the objects on our heap are marked, as we can tell by the 1 after every object. So, in our example, none of the objects is eligible for GC as they are all still reachable.

There are different algorithms that play an important role in the marking phase. The first one that we are going to have a look at is the stop-the-world approach.

Stop-the-world

Think about how this could be done for a second. While you are checking all the variables on the stack and marking all their objects and the nested objects, new objects could have been created in the meantime. It's possible that you missed that part of the stack. This would lead to unmarked objects (remember, objects are initially unmarked upon creation) that should have been marked, and they would be removed as a result. That would be very problematic.

The solution to this impacts performance as the garbage collector needs to pause the execution of the main application in order to make sure no new objects will be created during the marking phase. This strategy is called stop-the-world, which – as dramatic as it sounds – is a Java term. There also are other strategies in the field of computer science, one of them being reference counting, which we will look at next.

Reference counting and islands of isolation

Another implementation approach is of counting the number of references on an object. All objects would contain a count of the number of times they were referenced as some sort of property. This way, executing GC is nothing more than just removing all the objects with a 0 for the number of times they are referenced.

You might be thinking that this is a lot better than pausing the application, and so, why don't we use it? The answer to that is islands of isolation. This is not some modern-day social phenomenon; islands of isolation are objects that just reference each other without having a connection to the stack.

Let's explore the stack and heap for the following code sample. We have a Nest class in this example:

```
class Nest {
    private Nest;

    public Nest getNest() {
        return nest;
    }

    public void setNest(Nest nest) {
        this.nest = nest;
    }
}
```

We are creating two Nest instances and setting them to be each other's nest property:

```
public class IslandOfIsolation {
    public static void main(String[] args) {
        Nest n1 = new Nest(); // 1
        Nest n2 = new Nest(); // 2
        n1.setNest(n2); // 3
        n2.setNest(n1); // 4
        n1 = null; // 5
        n2 = null; // 6
    }
}
```

Let's have a look at what it would like to count the references and pause after line 4.

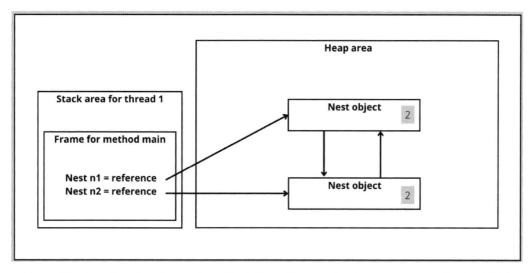

Figure 4.7 – Overview after the creation of both Nest objects and assigning them to each other's field

After line 4, both counters are 2. The objects are referenced by both the other object and the stack. This changes after line 5 and 6 since the references to the stack are removed.

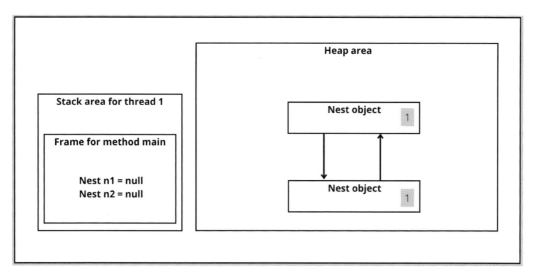

Figure 4.8 – Overview after setting the stack references to null

As you can tell by the code, after the execution of the line with comment 6 at the end, both objects are unreachable from the stack. However, if we would use the counting of the references, they would both still have a 1, since they are both referring to each other.

Since these objects don't have a 0 count but also do not have a connection to the stack. They are islands: islands of isolation. They should be garbage collected, but the simple counting garbage collector cannot detect them because they don't have a reference count of 0. The more advanced garbage collector, which marks all the elements with a connection to the stack that needs to pause the application, does garbage collect them, as they don't have a connection to the stack.

Therefore, Java uses the more-accurate marking phase to pause the application. Without the marking garbage collector, islands of isolation would lead to a memory leak: memory that could be released but is never made available for the application to use again.

Next, let's talk about how the memory is freed up after being marked.

Sweeping by the garbage collector

Once the objects that need to be kept are marked, it's time to start the next phase to actually free the memory. This deletion of the objects is called sweeping in GC jargon. To make it more interesting, we have three kinds of sweeping:

- Normal sweeping
- Sweeping with compacting
- Sweeping with copying

We are going to discuss all these in more detail with illustrations to help you understand what's going on.

Normal sweeping

Normal sweeping is the removal of unmarked objects. *Figure 4.9* shows five objects in memory. Two of them, the ones with an **x** in them, will be removed.

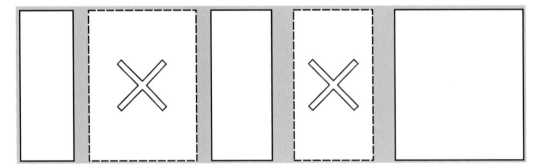

Figure 4.9 – Schematic overview of memory with marked objects

The memory blocks are not of equal sizes; some of them are smaller while others are larger. After sweeping the unreachable objects, the memory looks as follows:

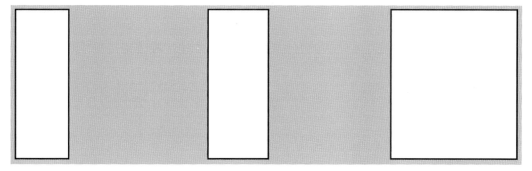

Figure 4.10 – Schematic overview of memory after sweeping

The memory has been freed up by the sweeping and the gaps in between the memory blocks can be allocated again. However, only blocks that fit in between the gaps can be stored there. The memory is now fragmented, and this can lead to problems with storing larger memory blocks.

Fragmentation

Fragmentation of memory happens after storing the memory first and then removing blocks from the middle. In between the memory blocks, new memory can be allocated. This is shown in *Figure 4.11*.

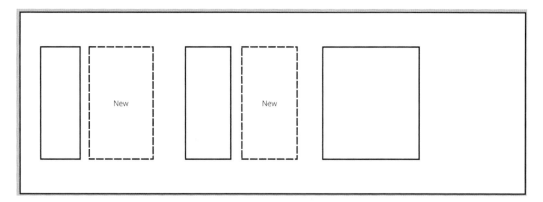

Figure 4.11 – Allocation of new objects in fragmented memory

The new memory blocks are stored in the gaps. This works well in the specific displayed situation, where the memory blocks fit the gaps. If the memory blocks don't fit in between the gaps (or at the end in this overview), we have a problem. Let's look at a situation where we want to store a new block.

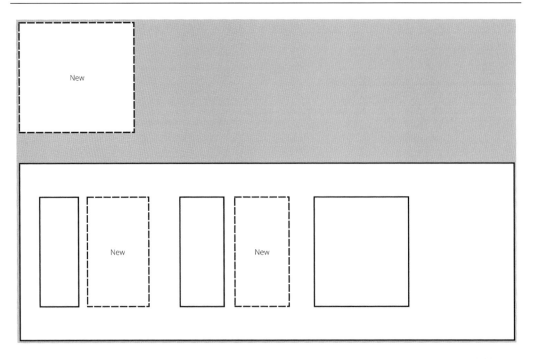

Figure 4.12 – Attempting to store a large block of memory that is less than the memory available

If we would look at the total memory available, the block seen in the preceding figure would fit. However, we cannot store it in the fragmented memory as there isn't enough contiguous memory available to store the new block.

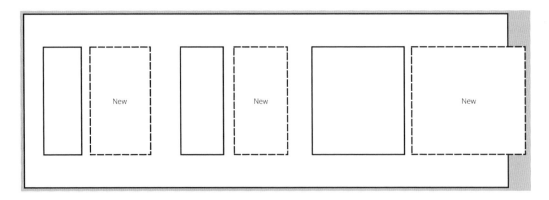

Figure 4.13 – Schematic overview that shows that the new memory block doesn't fit

Not being able to fit in a block of requested memory would lead to an error: OutOfMemoryError. Even though we are not out of memory and technically there is enough memory available to store the new block, it doesn't fit because the memory that's available is fragmented. This is a problem with normal sweeping. It is a very efficient and easy process, but it leads to fragmented memory. This process could be favorable if there is plenty of memory and the application just needs to free up memory fast. When memory is tighter, it is favorable to use one of the other options for sweeping: sweeping with compacting or sweeping with copying. Let's have a look at sweeping with compacting first.

Sweeping with compacting

Sweeping with compacting is a two-step process. Just like in normal sweeping, the memory blocks are deleted. This time, we do not accept the fragmented memory as the end result but execute an extra step called compacting. This moves the blocks of memory to ensure there are no gaps between them. The process is shown in *Figure 4.14*. We assume the same memory blocks are ready for removal, as shown in *Figure 4.9*.

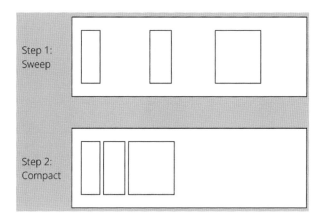

Figure 4.14 – Sweeping with compacting

As you can see, this time we do not end up with fragmented memory. Therefore, we will not get OutOfMemoryError. That sounds amazing, but as always, magic comes at a price. In this case, the price is performance. The compacting of the memory is a costly process in terms of performance, since all the memory blocks need to be moved (and this needs to happen mostly sequentially).

There is an alternative to this costly compacting process and that's sweeping with copying. Don't forget about sweeping with compacting just yet as sweeping with copying comes with its own cost.

Sweeping with copying

Sweeping with copying is a clever process. We need two memory regions for this. Instead of deleting the memory blocks we no longer need, we delete all the memory blocks! But not before we've copied the ones we still need to the second memory region (refer to *Figure 4.15*).

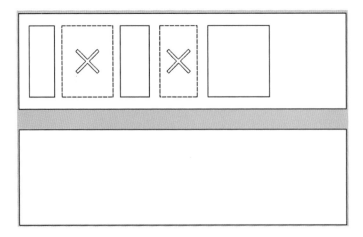

Figure 4.15 – Sweeping with copying before the actual sweeping

First, we have our memory region with the objects that are no longer needed, and then we have a second memory region that is not allocated yet.

In the next step, we copy all the objects we need to the second memory region.

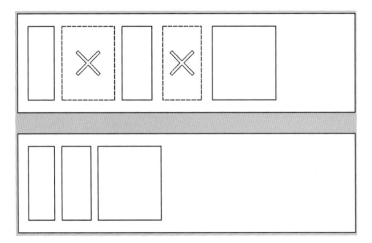

Figure 4.16 – Sweeping with copying after copying

So far, we have only copied and not swept anything yet. That's exactly what the next step is going to do: clear the first memory region, since all the objects we still need are kept in the second memory region. The result is shown in *Figure 4.17*.

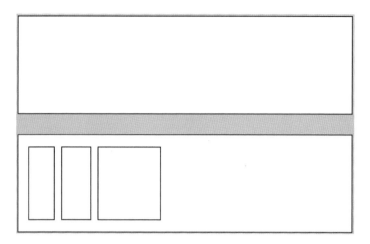

Figure 4.17 – Schematic overview of the memory after sweeping with copying

After sweeping the first memory region, we have all our objects that are still reachable in the second memory region. This is better in terms of performance than sweeping with compacting, but as you can imagine, this requires more free memory to be available.

Which types of sweeping are used depends on the selected implementation of the garbage collector. There are rather many implementations out there. We are going to explore the most common ones in the next section.

Exploring GC implementations

The standard JVM has five implementations for GC. Other Java implementations can have other GC implementations, such as the garbage collectors from IBM and Azul. The way these work is relatively easy to grasp after understanding the following five implementations that come with the standard JVM:

- Serial GC
- Parallel GC
- CMS (concurrent mark sweep) GC
- G1 GC
- ZGC (Z garbage collector)

We will examine in detail how these implementations work a little later (however, we will not be discussing all the different command-line options for each of them). But, before we discuss how these specific garbage collectors work, another concept needs to be addressed: the concept of generational GC.

Generational GC

If you have a large Java application running, pausing the entire program in order to wait for the garbage collector to have marked every single live object would be a performance nightmare. Luckily, they thought of something cleverer by making use of the different generations on the heap. Not all of the soon-to-be-explained garbage collectors use this strategy, but some of them do.

Instead of running a full garbage collector round at once, generational garbage collectors focus on a certain part of memory, for example, the young generation. This approach would work well for applications that have most of their objects die young. It saves a lot of marking.

The generational garbage collectors often work with a **remembered set**. This is a set that has all the references from objects to the young generation coming from the old generation. This way, the old generation does not need to be scanned since the references to the young generation are already in the remembered set.

Applications that have most of their objects in the tenured generation will not thrive with the approach of focusing on the young generation with their GC. Since, in this scenario, the heap is especially heavy on the old generation, only collecting the young generation will not free a high ratio of memory.

Often generational garbage collectors have to use different strategies for different memory areas. For example, the young generation could be garbage collected with a stop-the-world garbage collector that copies the entire set of reachable objects to the old generation and then deletes the young generation. Meanwhile, the old generation could work with compacting and perhaps an alternative to stop-the-world, such as the CMS garbage collector, which we'll see while going over the different implementations.

Now that we have discussed the different options for sweeping and both the stop-the-world and the generational garbage collector, we are in a better position to understand the five implementations that we listed earlier. (So, hold on, you've almost made it through this tough chapter!)

Serial GC

The **serial GC** runs on a single thread and uses the stop-the-world strategy. This means that the application is not running its main tasks when the garbage collector runs. It is the simplest option for garbage collection.

For the young generation, it uses the mark strategy to identify which objects are eligible for GC and the sweep with copying approach for the actual freeing of the memory. For the old generation, it uses the mark and sweep with compacting approach.

The serial garbage collector is ideal for small programs, but for larger programs such as **Spring** or **Quarkus** applications, there are better options.

Parallel GC

The **parallel garbage collector** is the default garbage collector of Java 8. It uses the mark-and-copy approach for the young generation and the mark-sweep-compact approach for the old generation, just like the serial garbage collector. However, and this might come as a surprise, it does so in parallel. In this case, parallel means that uses multiple threads to clean up the heap space. So, there is not one single thread taking care of the marking, copying, and compacting phases, but multiple threads. Even though it is still stop-the-world, it performs better than the serial garbage collector, since the world needs to be stopped for a shorter amount of time.

The parallel garbage collector will work well on machines with multiple cores. On (rarer) single-core machines, the serial garbage collector is probably a better choice, due to the costs of managing multiple threads and not really parallel processing on the single core.

CMS GC

The **Concurrent Mark Sweep Garbage Collector** (**CMS GC**) has an improved mark-and-sweep algorithm. It manages to do this with multiple threads and reduces the pause time drastically. This is the main difference between CMS GC and parallel garbage collector.

Not all systems can handle sharing resources between the main application and the garbage collector, though, but if they can, it is a great upgrade in terms of performance compared to the parallel garbage collector.

The CMS GC is a generational garbage collector as well. It has separate cycles for the young and old generation. For the young generation, it uses mark and copy with stop-the-world. So, during the GC of the young generation, the main application threads are paused.

The old generation is garbage collected with *mostly concurrent* mark and sweep. The term mostly concurrent means that it does most of the GC concurrently, but it will still use stop-the-world twice in a GC cycle. It pauses all the main application threads for the first time at the very beginning, then during the marking for a very short time, and then for a (usually) somewhat longer time around the middle of the GC cycle to do the final marking.

These pauses are typically very short, because the CMS GC attempts to collect enough of the old generation while running concurrently to the main application threads and, this way, prevent it from getting full. Sometimes, this is not possible. If the CMS GC cannot free up enough while the old generation is getting full, or the application fails to allocate an object, the CMS GC pauses all the application threads and the main focus shifts to GC. The situation in which this garbage collector fails to do the GC mostly concurrently is called *concurrent mode failure*.

If the collector then still cannot free up enough memory, `OutOfMemoryError` gets thrown. This happens when 98% of the application time is spent on GC and less than 2% of the heap is recovered.

This is not a lot different from the other garbage collectors that we've discussed. The very short pauses of the CMS GC sound pretty good already, but there are even later upgrades available. Let's have a look at the G1 GC.

G1 GC

The **G1** (**garbage-first**) garbage collector came with Java 7 (minor version 4) and is an upgrade of the CMS GC. It combines different algorithms in a clever way. The G1 collector is parallel, concurrent, and aims for short pauses of the application. It employs a technique called incrementally compacting.

The G1 garbage collector divides the heap into smaller regions: much smaller than the generational garbage collector. It works with these smaller memory segments to mark and sweep them. It keeps track of the amount of reachable and unreachable objects per memory region. The regions with the most unreachable objects are garbage collected first since that frees up the most memory. That's why it is called the garbage-first garbage collector. Regions with the most garbage are collected first.

It does all this while copying objects from one region to another region. This will result in freeing up the first region completely. This way the G1 GC kills two birds with one stone: achieving GC and compacting at the same time. This is why it is such an upgrade compared to earlier mentioned garbage collector.

The G1 GC is a great garbage collector. You may wonder whether this garbage collector manages to work without stop-the-world. No, the compacting still needs to happen this way. But due to the smaller regions, the pauses are much shorter.

Another new feature of the G1 GC garbage collector is *string deduplication*. This is literally what you'd think it is: the garbage collector runs a process to inspect the String objects. When it finds String objects that contain the same content but refer to different char arrays on the heap, they will be updated to both point to the same char array. This makes the other char array eligible for GC and this way, the memory usage is optimized. As if this wasn't exciting enough, it happens completely concurrently! This option will need to be enabled using the following command: -XX:+UseStringDeduplication.

Just like the CMS GC, the G1 GC tries to do a lot of the GC concurrently. So, the application threads don't need to be paused most of the time. However, if the G1 GC cannot free up enough memory and the application is allocating more than can be freed up concurrently, the application threads need to be paused.

The G1 garbage collector is the go-to GC for powerful systems that are high performing and have a large memory space. This is not the most recently added garbage collector though. Let's have a look at the ZGC.

Z GC

Java 15 gave us yet another production-ready implementation of the garbage collector, the **Z garbage collector** (**ZGC**). It does all the garbage collecting concurrently and does not need to pause the application for more than 10 ms per pause.

It manages to do this by starting with marking the live objects. It doesn't keep a map but uses **reference coloring**. Reference coloring means that the live state of reference is stored as the bits that are part of the reference. This requires some extra bits, which is why the ZGC only works on 64-bit systems and not on 32-bit systems.

Fragmentation is avoided by using relocation. This process happens in parallel with the application in order to avoid pauses of more than 10 ms, but this happens while the application is being executed.

Without extra measurements, this could lead to unpleasant surprises. Imagine that we were trying to access a certain object with the reference, but while doing so, it got relocated and has a new reference. The old memory location could be overwritten or cleared already. In such a scenario, debugging would be a nightmare.

Of course, the Java team would not push a garbage collector to production with issues like that. They introduced load barriers to deal with this. The load barriers run whenever a reference from the heap is loaded. It checks the metadata bits of the reference and, based on the result, it may or may not do some processing before retrieving the result. This magic is called remapping.

The five garbage collectors we've just discussed are the main options to choose from at the moment of writing this book. Your options depend on the Java version that you're using, the system configuration, and the type of application. In order to make sure the garbage collector performs well, monitoring should be in place. This is exactly what we're going to look at in the next section.

Monitoring GC

In order to decide upon the right garbage collector, you'll need to know your application. There are a few metrics that are especially important for the GC:

- **Allocation rate**: How fast the application allocates objects in memory.
- **Heap population**: The number of objects and their size living on the heap.
- **Mutation rate**: How often references are updated in memory.
- **Average object live time**: The time the objects live on average. One application may have objects that die young, while another application may have objects that live longer.

The monitoring of the performance of the GC requires different metrics. The most important ones are mark time, compaction time, and GC cycle time. The mark time entails the time it takes the garbage collector to find all the live objects on the heap. Compaction time is how long it takes the garbage collector to free up all the space and relocate the objects. The GC cycle time is how long it takes the garbage collector to perform a full GC.

Whenever there is little heap space available, you'll see the CPU usage for GC increase. Choosing the right amount of memory will improve the performance of your application. The greater the amount of available memory, the easier the garbage collector can function.

The copy-and-compact collector needs to have enough space available for copying and relocating. This is a much more costly process when available memory is limited. Only a small memory segment could be copied to free up a bit more so that hopefully a bit more can be copied next time, and so on. The CPU usage of the garbage collector is the highest on low memory. On the other end of the spectrum, in the hypothetical situation that we would have unlimited memory, we wouldn't really need to garbage collect at all.

In *Chapter 6*, we're going to have a look at the usage of JVM tuning for memory management to improve the functioning of the JVM memory. There, we'll also see how we can tune a garbage collector.

Summary

In this chapter, we have seen how the GC of the heap works in more depth. Objects on the heap are eligible for GC when they don't have a connection to the stack anymore, whether directly or indirectly.

The garbage collector determines which objects are eligible for GC in the marking phase. Objects that have a connection to the stack are marked. The objects that are eligible for GC are unmarked.

After this marking phase, the actual removal happens in the sweeping phase. We discussed three kinds of sweeping, normal sweeping, sweeping with compacting, and sweeping with copying.

Then, we discussed the different implementations of the garbage collectors. A subset of them are the generational garbage collectors. These garbage collectors focus on one of the generations of the heap and, consequently, do not need to scan all the objects of the heap during the marking phase. After that, we discussed five common implementations of the garbage collector.

In the next chapter, we're going to zoom in on the Metaspace.

5

Zooming in on the Metaspace

In *Chapter 4*, we examined garbage collection in detail. We discovered that objects without a reference are eligible for garbage collection. In effect, the garbage collector marks the objects that have a connection back to the stack, annotating them as live objects. The sweep phase of the garbage collector then reclaims the memory of the objects that are not marked (the dead objects).

We also examined the various garbage collection implementations. Based on your specific criteria, an evaluation of each implementation is required.

This chapter focuses on an area known as the **Metaspace**. We will examine the Metaspace under the following headings:

- JVM usage of the Metaspace
- Class loading
- Releasing Metaspace memory

Let us start with the JVM usage of the Metaspace.

JVM usage of the Metaspace

The Metaspace is a special area of native memory outside of the heap. Native memory is memory provided by the operating system to an application for its own use. The JVM uses the Metaspace to store class-related information, that is, the class's runtime representation. This is the class's metadata; hence the *meta*data is stored in the *Meta*space.

> **Metadata**
> Metadata is information about data. For example, columns in a database are metadata about the data in the columns. Thus, if a column name is Name and a specific row value is John, then Name is metadata about John.

This metadata consists of the following:

- Class files

- Structure and methods of the class

- Constants

- Annotations

- Optimizations

Thus, in metadata, the JVM has everything it requires to work with the class.

> **PermGen**
>
> Prior to Java 8, the metadata was stored in an area (contiguous with the heap) known as **PermGen**, or **permanent generation**. PermGen stored the class metadata, interned strings, and the class's static variables. As of Java 8, the class metadata is now stored in the Metaspace, and interned strings and class/static variables are stored on the heap.

Let us now examine class loading.

Class loading

When a class is accessed for the first time (for example, when an object of the class is created), the class loader locates the class file and allocates its metadata in the Metaspace. The class loader owns this allocated Metaspace and the class loader instance itself is loaded onto the heap. Once loaded, subsequent references reuse the metadata of that same class.

There are two class loaders worth mentioning at this point: the bootstrap class loader (which is responsible for loading the class loaders themselves) and the application class loader. Both of these class loaders' metadata reside permanently in Metaspace and consequently, are never garbage collected. Dynamic class loaders (and the classes they load) are, on the other hand, eligible for garbage collection.

This leads us to the release of memory from the Metaspace.

Releasing Metaspace memory

One of the major changes from PermGen (pre-Java 8) to Metaspace (Java 8 onwards) is that the Metaspace can now grow in size. By default, the amount of memory allocated for the Metaspace is unbounded, as it is part of native memory. The size of the Metaspace can be customized using the JVM `-XX:MetaspaceSize` flag.

The Metaspace can trigger garbage collection in only two scenarios:

- Metaspace runs out of memory
- Metaspace size exceeds a JVM-set threshold

Let us examine these in turn.

Metaspace runs out of memory

As stated, by default, the native memory available to the Metaspace is unlimited. If you run out of memory, you get an `OutOfMemoryError` message, and this will trigger a run of the garbage collector. You can limit the Metaspace size with the JVM `-XX:MaxMetaspaceSize` flag. If you reach this limit, that will also trigger a run of the garbage collector.

Metaspace size exceeds a JVM-set threshold

We can configure the JVM to trigger a garbage collection when the Metaspace reaches a certain threshold, known as the **high-water mark**. In addition, we can adjust this threshold dynamically based on garbage collection results. Raising the high-water mark prevents inducing another garbage collection too quickly. Lowering the high-water mark does the opposite; it helps induce another garbage collection more quickly. The threshold or high-water mark is initially set to the value of the JVM `-XX:MetaspaceSize` flag. We use the `-XX:MinMetaspaceFreeRatio` and `-XX:MaxMetaspaceFreeRatio` flags to raise or lower the high-water mark, respectively.

Now that we know when garbage collection runs in the Metaspace, let us examine how garbage collection works regarding the Metaspace.

Garbage collection of the Metaspace

As the class loader owns the metadata for a class, the garbage collector can only reclaim this metadata when the class loader itself is dead. The class loader is only dead when there are no instances of any classes loaded by that loader.

Let us look at an example to help explain this further. The example assumes a dynamic class loader and uses simplified diagrams for ease of explanation.

Figure 5.1 details the situation in memory after we have created two objects of the **O** type and one object of the **P** type.

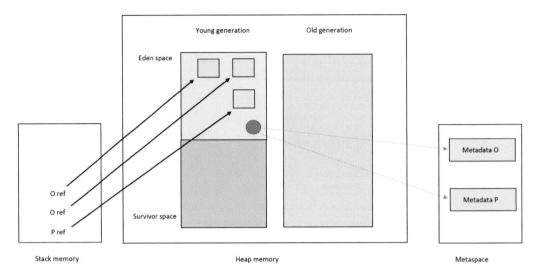

Figure 5.1 – Metaspace allocation

In the preceding figure, initially, the JVM creates the class loader object (dark blue), two objects of the **O** type (light blue), and one object of the **P** type (yellow) on the heap. The **O** and **P** references are on the stack. Upon creating the first **O** and **P** instances, the class loader loads the metadata for both **O** and **P** in the Metaspace. However, when creating the second instance of **O**, nothing happens in the Metaspace because the metadata for **O** is already loaded.

Figure 5.2 will show the situation in memory when both of the **O** references go out of scope but garbage collection has not yet run:

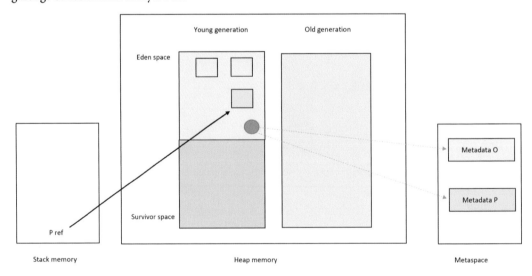

Figure 5.2 – Metaspace (both O references out of scope)

As you can see, the JVM has popped both of the **O** references from the stack. Garbage collection has not yet run so the instances remain on the heap. *Figure 5.3* shows the situation after the first run of garbage collection:

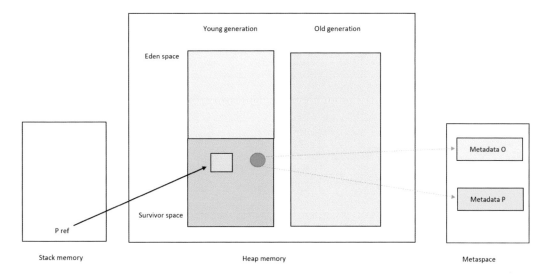

Figure 5.3 – Metaspace after garbage collection (run #1)

In the preceding figure, we can see that the garbage collector reclaimed the two (dead) **O** objects from the heap. In addition, the garbage collector moved both the class loader and **P** objects to the survivor space.

Note that the metadata for **O** remains in the Metaspace even though no objects of the **O** type are on the heap. This is because the garbage collector could not reclaim the class loader for **O** due to the existence of the object of the **P** type on the heap (the same class loader loaded both **O** and **P**).

Figure 5.4 shows the situation in memory when the **P** reference goes out of scope and garbage collection runs again:

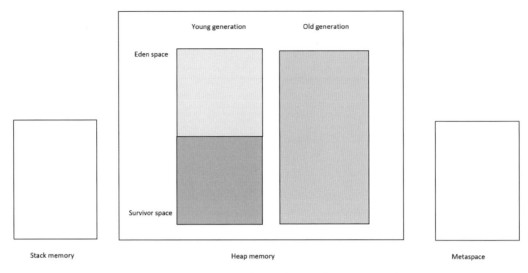

Figure 5.4 – Metaspace after garbage collection (run #2)

We can see that the JVM has popped the reference of **P** from the stack. As a result, the garbage collector reclaimed the object of the **P** type.

As the garbage collector has now reclaimed all instances of **O** and **P** types, it can reclaim the class loader that loaded **O** and **P**. Now, finally, the garbage collector can reclaim the metadata for **O** and **P** classes in the Metaspace.

That wraps up this chapter. Let us recap the major points.

Summary

In this chapter, we zoomed in on the Metaspace (formerly known as PermGen). The Metaspace is a special area of non-heap memory reserved for a class's metadata. The metadata consists of information enabling the JVM to work with the class: for example, method bytecode, constants, and annotations. When a class is first used, its metadata is loaded into the Metaspace. An example is the creation of an object for the first time.

By default, the native memory available to the Metaspace is unlimited. A maximum Metaspace size is configurable using the JVM `-XX:MaxMetaspaceSize` flag. A threshold value or high-water mark can be set initially using the `-XX:MetaspaceSize` flag. If a threshold value is set and reached, this induces a run of the garbage collector. Using both JVM flags, `-XX:MinMetaspaceFreeRatio` and `-XX:MaxMetaspaceFreeRatio`, in conjunction with garbage collection results, we can dynamically influence the high-water mark and, therefore, the interval to the next run of the garbage collector.

We saw, using an example, how the metadata for a class remains in Metaspace until the garbage collector deallocates the class loader that loaded that class. This cannot occur until all classes loaded by that class loader have no instances.

Now that we have zoomed in on the Metaspace, we will turn our attention to the next chapter, which focuses on configuring and monitoring the memory management of the JVM.

6

Configuring and Monitoring the Memory Management of the JVM

So far, we have looked at the different areas of memory and how it is deallocated, but we have yet to look at optimizing the way a **Java Virtual Machine** (**JVM**) does this. The approach that the JVM uses to manage memory can be configured in different ways.

There is not one obvious way to configure the JVM though. The best configuration really depends on the application and the requirements. Getting the best configuration will improve the performance of your application and minimize the memory requirements. Monitoring performance and memory will help discover problems before users do.

In this chapter, we're going to have a look at how to configure the JVM and monitor memory management. Changing the configurations of the JVM is typically done by tuning, meaning that you have an idea of where to start, then make small adjustments, and carefully measure their impact. Here are the topics that will be discussed:

- The basics of JVM tuning for memory management
- Obtaining relevant metrics for memory management
- Profiling of the Java application
- Tuning the configurations of the JVM

Technical requirements

The code for this chapter can be found on GitHub at `https://github.com/PacktPublishing/B18762_Java-Memory-Management`.

The basics of JVM tuning for memory management

The first rule of JVM tuning for performance improvement is probably that it should be the last option for improvement. Look at this code snippet:

```
int i = 0;
List<Integer> list = new ArrayList<>();
while(i < 100) {
    list.add((int)Math.ceil(Math.random()*1000));
}
```

Will JVM tuning help? No, because we're stuck in an infinite loop, since i never gets increased. Of course, there are a lot of less obvious examples, but when code can be improved and optimized, this must be done first before thinking about JVM tuning.

If the hardware can realistically be optimized, this should be done before JVM tuning as well. By this, I don't mean that you should fix a memory leak by just adding more memory; of course, that's not a fix. But when your application accidentally gets very successful and things get slow, chances are that you are better off upgrading the hardware than diving into JVM tuning to fix this. When all the other factors that come into play for performance are optimized, this is when JVM tuning can be applied for performance improvement.

When we are tuning the JVM, we are setting parameters. And that's not it; this needs to be carefully monitored. Before changing any settings, we must make sure to have a good idea of the metrics of our application. These new settings need to be monitored carefully. If the performance improves, you could try to change the parameters a bit more; if it gets worse, you should probably change it back at least a little to gauge the difference.

It might sound like trial and error at this point, and to some extent it is – professionally conducted trial and error, that is. Let's have a look at the relevant metrics to tune the memory management of the JVM.

Obtaining relevant metrics for memory management

There are several important metrics for knowing how the memory of an application is doing. Understanding the following three important concepts that define the performance of the application is the first step here:

- Memory that is functioning well
- Normal latency
- A normal level of throughput

Let's take a look at each one of these.

Well-functioning memory

When you have experience with a specific application, you may know its stable memory-usage point. There needs to be more memory available than just the stable usage point though. Instead, a safe amount of memory needs to be available for the Java application, and this reserved memory should not be almost full. Conversely, having too much memory allocated for the Java application is also not the way to go. This is because the rest of the system will also need some memory for other processes, since the operating system is also running.

If you have an idea of the normal memory metrics of your application when it's performing well, this will help you measure the outcome of any adjustments that you might be making later.

Normal latency

Latency is also called the responsiveness of the application. An application with normal latency responds as expected and required. This can be measured in time – for example, the time the application takes to process a certain request such as processing an incoming HTTP request.

Of course, measuring latency is not always as easy. If we have a standalone Java application, this is somewhat trivial. We know that we are measuring the latency of our application. If we are trying to measure the latency of an enterprise application, it becomes tricky. We need to make sure we are measuring the latency of our application and not network issues, the server side of another application, or any layer that we have in our enterprise application landscape. In those cases, issues with the latency results are likely not related to the memory management of our application.

Level of throughput

Throughput is the amount of work that can be done by the application in a certain amount of time. High throughput is typically what you want to aim for, but it does require more memory and might affect latency.

Profiling Java applications

Profiling is used to make an analysis of the runtime performance of an application. This is something that needs to be done carefully, since it usually has an impact on the application that is being profiled. It is, therefore, advisable to profile the development environment if possible. We are going to have a look at profiling with the `jstat` and `jmap` command-line tools, and the **VisualVM** application. The first two come with your **Java Development Kit** (**JDK**); the latter used to come with it but now it can be downloaded separately.

> **Important note**
> You can download VisualVM here: `https://visualvm.github.io/download.html`.

There are other profiles out there; some IDEs even have their own profilers built in, which work in a similar way.

Profiling with jstat and jmap

With the two command-line utilities, jstat and jmap, we can analyze and profile memory. We are going to explore how to do that.

Let's say we have a simple Java application:

```
package chapter6;

import java.util.ArrayList;
import java.util.List;

public class ExampleAnalysis {
    public static List<String> stringList = new ArrayList<>();
    public static void main(String[] args) {
        for(int i = 0; i < 1000000000; i++) {
            stringList.add("String " + i);
            System.out.println(stringList.get(i));
        }
    }
}
```

This application is not doing a lot of interesting things, just adding a lot of String objects to our stringList static list.

We can run this program and see what is going on with the memory. In order to do this, we need to compile the program first:

```
javac ExampleAnalysis.java
```

The preceding command assumes that you are in the same folder as Command Prompt or Terminal, since we access the file directly without any folders in front. This command compiles the code and stores the result in ExampleAnalysis.class. Let's run this file by executing the following command (make sure to be one level above the Chapter 6 directory):

```
java chapter6.ExampleAnalysis
```

Now, we'll first need the process ID to analyze our code using `jstat`. We can get the process IDs of all Java processes by running the following command in the command line:

```
jps
```

The command produces the following output:

```
35169  Launcher
35397  Jps
30565
35384  ExampleAnalysis
34846
```

Our program can be easily recognized, as it has the name of the class written after it. So, our process ID is `35384`.

We need this process ID to run the `jstat` analysis. This command-line tool has several options. We are going to start by running it like this:

```
jstat -gc -t 35384 1000 10
```

This will produce the result for our process with an ID of `35384`. The `-gc` option is one of the options available to get statistics about the garbage collected heap. It makes sure that it shows the behavior of the garbage collected heap. There are a few other flags that you could use as well; here are a few examples:

- `gccapacity`: Show data about the capacities of the generations
- `gcnew`: Show data about the behavior of the young generations
- `gcnewcapacity`: Show data about the size of the young generations
- `gcold`: Show data about the old generation and the Metaspace
- `gcoldcapacity`: Show data about the old generation
- `gcutil`: Show a summary of the garbage collection data

`-t` indicates that it should print the timestamp. `1000` means that it will show the statistics every 1,000 milliseconds and `10` means that it will show 10 iterations.

The output will look as shown in *Figure 6.1*:

```
maaikes-mbp:~ maaikevanputten$ jstat -gc -t 32822 1000 10
Timestamp        S0C       S1C       S0U       S1U         EC        EU        OC        OU        MC
       MU    CCSC     CCSU     YGC     YGCT    FGC    FGCT    CGC    CGCT      GCT
       20,8      0,0    8192,0      0,0    8192,0    49152,0    28672,0    475136,0    74301,0    448,0
   233,8    128,0      6,0      4    0,042      0    0,000      0    0,000    0,042
       21,8      0,0    8192,0      0,0    8192,0    49152,0    36864,0    475136,0    74301,0    448,0
   233,8    128,0      6,0      4    0,042      0    0,000      0    0,000    0,042
       22,8      0,0    8192,0      0,0    8192,0    57344,0     4096,0    466944,0    96272,5    448,0
   233,8    128,0      6,0      5    0,057      0    0,000      0    0,000    0,057
       23,8      0,0    8192,0      0,0    8192,0    57344,0    12288,0    466944,0    96272,5    448,0
   233,8    128,0      6,0      5    0,057      0    0,000      0    0,000    0,057
       24,8      0,0    8192,0      0,0    8192,0    57344,0    16384,0    466944,0    96272,5    448,0
   233,8    128,0      6,0      5    0,057      0    0,000      0    0,000    0,057
       25,8      0,0    8192,0      0,0    8192,0    57344,0    24576,0    466944,0    96272,5    448,0
   233,8    128,0      6,0      5    0,057      0    0,000      0    0,000    0,057
       26,8      0,0    8192,0      0,0    8192,0    57344,0    32768,0    466944,0    96272,5    448,0
   233,8    128,0      6,0      5    0,057      0    0,000      0    0,000    0,057
       27,8      0,0    8192,0      0,0    8192,0    57344,0    36864,0    466944,0    96272,5    448,0
   233,8    128,0      6,0      5    0,057      0    0,000      0    0,000    0,057
       28,8      0,0    8192,0      0,0    8192,0    57344,0    45056,0    466944,0    96272,5    448,0
   233,8    128,0      6,0      5    0,057      0    0,000      0    0,000    0,057
       29,8      0,0    8192,0      0,0    8192,0    73728,0        0,0    450560,0   137312,0    448,0
   233,8    128,0      6,0      6    0,073      0    0,000      0    0,000    0,073
```

Figure 6.1 – Output showing the jstat command with options

As you can see, it displays many columns. Let us see what these columns mean; the exact values aren't too important for the discussion. We'll go over them from left to right:

- **Timestamp**: The time since the program started running. You can see that it increases with seconds, which makes sense, as we asked for iterations of 1,000 milliseconds.

- **S0C**: The current capacity of the survivor space 0 in KB.

- **S1C**: The current capacity of the survivor space 1 in KB.

- **S0U**: The part of the survivor space 0 that is being used in KB.

- **S1U**: The part of the survivor space 1 that is being used in KB.

- **EC**: The current capacity of the Eden space in KB. You can see that the capacity scales up when the Eden space gets fuller.

- **EU**: The part of the Eden space that is being used in KB. At the seventh row, it drops, and the data gets moved to the old space.

- **OC**: The current capacity of the old space in KB.

- **OU**: The part of the old space that is being used in KB. You can see it increase during the program.

- **MC**: The current capacity of the Metaspace in KB.

- **MU**: The part of the Metaspace that is being used in KB.

- **CCSC: Compressed Class Space Capacity** in KB.

- **CCSU: Compressed Class Space Utilized** in KB.
- **YGC:** The number of young generation garbage collection events that happened.
- **YGCT:** The total time of the young generation garbage collection events.
- **FGC:** The total number of full garbage collection events.
- **FGCT:** The total time the full garbage collection events took.
- **CGC: Concurrent Garbage Collection.**
- **CGCT:** The total time of concurrent garbage collection.
- **GCT:** The total garbage collection time.

With the `jmap` command, we can get more insights into the heap memory usage of our current process. Here is how to use it (Java 9 and later):

```
jhsdb jmap --heap --pid 35384
```

`jhsdb` is a JDK tool that can attach to a running Java process, perform snapshot debugging, and inspect the content of the core dump of a crashed JVM. This outputs the current heap configuration and usage. Let's have a look at how to get a more visual result while Java profiling with the help of VisualVM.

Profiling with VisualVM

There are many profilers out there that will give a visual representation of memory. One of them is VisualVM. It is a tool that is suitable for getting detailed information about the Java applications that are running. VisualVM does not come by default with the JDK anymore, so it needs to be installed separately here: `https://visualvm.github.io/`.

If your IDE supports profiling, you could work with that one too. However, the following examples use VisualVM, since it's a free tool that can be easily downloaded. Profiling an application with VisualVM is easy. First, you start VisualVM. You will see a screen similar to the one in *Figure 6.2*.

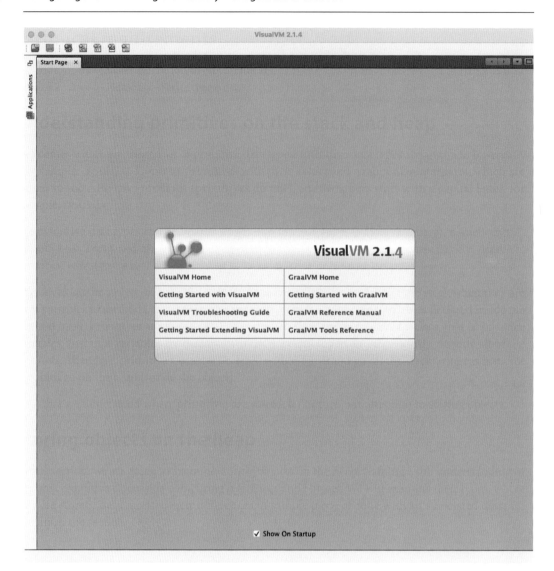

Figure 6.2 – The startup screen of VisualVM

On the screen of *Figure 6.2*, we can check the applications that are running. The **Applications** tab can be found on the top left, positioned vertically. Here, we can see the local Java processes that are running, from where we can simply select the one that we need. Let's start our example Java application, where we will create a huge list of strings.

In the **Applications** tab, we can see the processes, as shown in *Figure 6.3*.

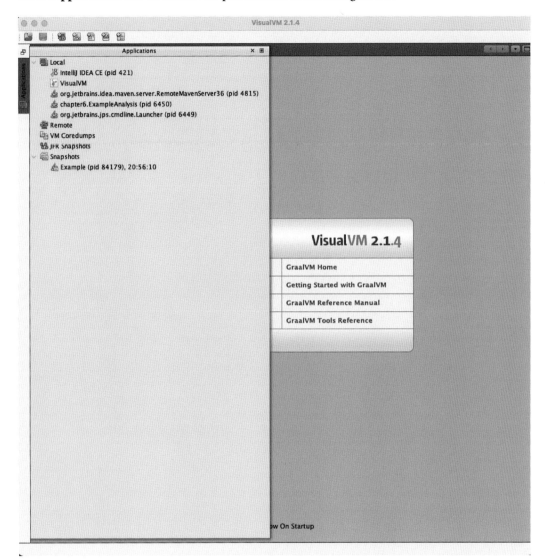

Figure 6.3 – An overview of the Java processes

We can now pick the process we want to examine. In this case, we would like to analyze the process with the **6450** PID. Once we click on it, we get an overview of the process, as shown in *Figure 6.4*.

Figure 6.4 – An overview of the Java process

We can see a summary of the data in the overview shown in *Figure 6.4*. We see the process that we are analyzing, the JVM and Java version that we are running, and the JVM arguments used to start the application. There is also a lot more detailed data we can get from VisualVM. At the top, we have several tabs: **Overview**, **Monitor**, **Threads**, **Sampler**, and **Profiler**. We have seen the **Overview** tab; in *Figure 6.5*, let's look at the data under the **Monitor** tab.

Figure 6.5 – Monitoring the Java process using VisualVM

This is where we get some serious details of what is going on in our application. We see four graphs. The top-left one shows **CPU usage**, and as you can see, we are using quite a bit of CPU for this program. This graph also shows the garbage collection activity, which is very low overall. This makes sense, as there is not a lot to be garbage-collected anyway. The garbage collection activity combined with the memory graph at the top right gives some great insights into how healthy our application is in terms of memory. If the garbage collector works really hard (as you can see, there is a lot of GC activity in the top-left graph) and the memory keeps increasing (the lower line representing **Used heap** in the top-right graph), it means that we are having a problem with a memory leak. Basically, if there are too frequent GC cycles, then it is an indication that you need to do some digging to see whether there is something wrong with GC and memory. After doing that, if there are still too frequent GC cycles and memory is also not coming down, then it is a red alert and you must investigate. In fact, **OutOfMemoryError: GC Overhead limit exceeded** is thrown by the JVM if it is spending more than 98% of the time on GC and recovering less than 2% of the heap.

The two bottom graphs show the loaded Java classes (left) and the threads in the application (right). We can get more details on threads by moving to the **Threads** tab. In *Figure 6.6*, we see an overview of the threads in our application.

Figure 6.6 – Threads in our application

We can see the name of our threads on the far left. The bars indicate what the state of our threads is over time – for example, running or waiting. We can then see the time they have been running.

In the **Sampler** tab, shown in *Figure 6.7*, we can see how the CPU or memory is doing.

Figure 6.7 – The Sampler tab in VisualVM

We are now looking at memory sampling, which shows how many live objects there are and how much space is being occupied by a certain class. Here, the `byte` array is the biggest one. This makes sense because the value of a string is stored in a byte array. You can also filter this overview per thread or have a look at how the CPU is performing.

In the last tab, we can see profiling. Profiling and sampling are used for similar purposes, but the process is different. Sampling is done by making thread dumps and analyzing these thread dumps. Profiling requires adding a bit of logic to an application so that it gives a signal when something happens. This affects the performance of the application quite a bit. Therefore, this is not something you'd want to be doing on applications that are running in production. It can give a lot of insights though.

You can see the result of profiling all the classes in *Figure 6.8*. Here, you can see a similar result to what we were getting for the sampling (though it had fewer objects being allocated at that point in time). In this case, sampling would have worked just as well.

VisualVM is great to get quick, visual insights on what is going on with the memory of your application. This is going to be especially useful while tuning the JVM and checking the results. In the next section, we are going to do exactly that – learn how to adjust the configuration of the JVM and see the impact of these adjustments.

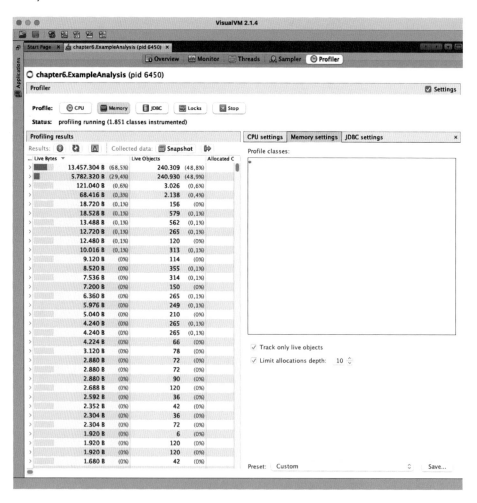

Figure 6.8 – Profiling all the classes

Tuning the configurations of the JVM

The settings of JVM can be adjusted. The process of adjusting the settings of JVM is called **tuning**. The idea of these adjustments is to boost the performance of the JVM. Once again, tuning should not be the first step in improving performance. Good code should always come first.

We are going to have a look at the settings that are related to memory management: the heap size, Metaspace, and the garbage collector.

Tuning the heap size and thread stack size

The heap size can be changed. It is generally best practice to not set the heap size to more than half of what is available on the server. This could lead to performance issues, as the server will be having other processes running as well.

The default size depends on the system. This command will show the defaults on a Windows system:

```
java -XX:+PrintFlagsFinal -version | findstr HeapSize
```

This command shows the default output for a macOS system:

```
java -XX:+PrintFlagsFinal -version | grep HeapSize
```

The output is displayed in bytes. You can see the output for my computer in *Figure 6.9*.

```
maaikes-mbp:~ maaikevanputten$ java -XX:+PrintFlagsFinal -version | grep HeapSize
    size_t ErgoHeapSizeLimit                       = 0                         {product} {default}
    size_t HeapSizePerGCThread                     = 43620760                  {product} {default}
    size_t InitialHeapSize                         = 536870912                 {product} {ergonomic}
    size_t LargePageHeapSizeThreshold              = 134217728                 {product} {default}
    size_t MaxHeapSize                             = 8589934592                {product} {ergonomic}
    size_t MinHeapSize                             = 8388608                   {product} {ergonomic}
     uintx NonNMethodCodeHeapSize                  = 5839372                {pd product} {ergonomic}
     uintx NonProfiledCodeHeapSize                 = 122909434              {pd product} {ergonomic}
     uintx ProfiledCodeHeapSize                    = 122909434              {pd product} {ergonomic}
    size_t SoftMaxHeapSize                         = 8589934592             {manageable} {ergonomic}
openjdk version "18.0.1.1" 2022-04-22
OpenJDK Runtime Environment (build 18.0.1.1+2-6)
OpenJDK 64-Bit Server VM (build 18.0.1.1+2-6, mixed mode, sharing)
```

Figure 6.9 – Output as seen on the macOS system

The size of the heap influences garbage collection. This might seem counterintuitive at first, but let's do a little thought experiment here. If we had unlimited heap memory, would we need garbage collection? No, right? Why run such an expensive process if we don't need to free up memory anyway?

The smaller the heap, the more we will need the garbage collector active because it would need to work harder to have space available, since memory gets filled up easier. However, the bigger the heap, the longer one full cycle of garbage collection takes. There's simply more to scan for garbage. A good rule of thumb is that you want to have less than 5% of application execution time spent on garbage collection.

The actual tuning works differently for different servers. Here, we are going to see how to do so using the command line when starting the application. Please note that the names of the options that we are setting are the same between different servers, but how or where to set them might vary.

When we start the Java application, we can work with different options for the memory. We can specify a memory pool start size, a maximum memory pool, and the thread stack size. Here's how to set all to 1,024 MB:

- `-Xms1024m` (initial size heap)
- `-Xmx1024m` (maximum size heap)
- `-Xss1024m` (thread stack size)

If you want to set it to a different size, choose a different size and just adjust the option accordingly. You can use the following command to start a Java application with adjusted memory settings (on a 64-bit system):

```
java -Xms4g -Xmx6g ExampleAnalysis
```

This will start our example Java application with an initial heap size of 4 GB and a maximum of 6 GB.

Similar to the way you can bind the total heap size using `-Xmx` and `-Xms`, you can bind the young generation size using the following:

- `-XX:MaxNewSize=1024m` (maximum new size)
- `-XX:NewSize=1024m` (minimum new size)

Here, we are setting the minimum and the maximum size to 1,024 MB. We may run out of memory. This will result in `OutOfMemoryError`. Let's see how to get a heap dump when this happens so that we can inspect what went wrong.

Logging low memory

It is very helpful to get a **heap dump** when an application ends with an out-of-memory error. A heap dump is a snapshot of the objects in the memory of the application. In this case, we can inspect the objects in the application that were present at the moment we ran out of memory. This way, we can use it to see which object is likely to overflow the memory.

If you want the JVM to create the heap dump whenever there is an `OutOfMemoryError` exception, then you can use the following JVM argument while starting the JVM:

```
java -XX:+HeapDumpOnOutOfMemoryError ExampleAnalysis
```

We can also specify the path:

```
java -XX:+HeapDumpOnOutOfMemoryError -XX:HeapDumpPath=/some/
path/to/dumps ExampleAnalysis
```

With this, the heap dumps will be stored in the specified path. There are different ways to create a heap dump – for example, `jmap` can also be used to create a heap dump of the application, if it didn't crash because of `OutOfMemoryError`.

Next, let's see how to configure the Metaspace.

Tuning the Metaspace

The default behavior of Metaspace is quite peculiar, as it seems to have a limit. This is easy to interpret in the wrong way because this limit is not a real limit. If it reaches this limit, it will see what it can do in terms of garbage collection, and then it expands. Therefore, it is important to set the following variables carefully:

- Maximum size, using `-XX:MaxMetaspaceSize=2048m`
- Threshold for garbage collection, using `-XX:MetaspaceSize=1024m`
- Minimum and maximum free ratio, using the following:

  - `-XX:MinMetaspaceFreeRatio=50`
  - `-XX:MaxMetaspaceFreeRatio=50`

The minimum and maximum free ratios are great for when you are planning to load a lot of classes dynamically. By making sure there is enough memory available, you can increase the speed to load classes dynamically. This is because the freeing up of memory for classes that need to be loaded takes some CPU time. We can skip the step that requires assigning additional memory by choosing a large enough free ratio and making sure memory is available. In the preceding example, they are set to 50%.

Garbage collection tuning

As you may have realized by now, garbage collection is an expensive process. Optimizing it can really help the performance of an application. You cannot trigger garbage collection yourself; this is the decision of the JVM. You may have heard of the following way to suggest garbage collection to the JVM:

```
System.gc();
```

This does not guarantee that garbage collection will take place. So, you cannot trigger garbage collection, but you can influence the way the JVM deals with it.

However, before tweaking anything in relation to garbage collection, it is important to make sure that you understand what you are doing exactly. For this, you'll need solid knowledge about the garbage collector.

Also, before adjusting anything, you must have a look at memory usage. Make sure to know what spaces are filled and when this is happening. A heap that's healthy will look a bit like a saw in VisualVM. It goes up and down, creating spikes, resembling the teeth of a saw. It has a certain amount of used memory, and then the garbage collection comes around and decreases the used memory to a certain base level. It grows again, and then at around the same usage level, the garbage collection comes around and decreases it to its base level, and so on.

If you see the memory growing over time and garbage collection ends at a slightly higher base level every time, you probably have a memory leak that needs to be dealt with. As we saw in *Chapter 4*, there are several different garbage collector implementations available. When starting the JVM, we can also choose which garbage collector we want it to use:

- `-XX:+UseSerialGC`

- `-XX:-UseParallelGC`

- `-XX:+UseConcMarkSweepGC`

- `-XX:+G1GC`

- `-XX:+UseZGC`

This is not possible for every system, and all these garbage collection choices come with their own extra options as well. For example, we can choose the parallel garbage collector and specify the number of threads for the garbage collector:

```
java -XX:+UseParallelGC -XX:ParallelGCThreads=4 ExampleAnalysis
```

This is how to start an application using the parallel garbage collector and giving it four threads to work with. The options for all the garbage collectors are too elaborate to discuss in detail. Details can be found in the official documentation of the Java implementation that you are using. Here is the link to the Oracle implementation, although it's possible that newer versions will have been released by the time you are reading this book: https://docs.oracle.com/javase/9/gctuning/introduction-garbage-collection-tuning.htm.

Summary

In this chapter, we saw what to keep in mind when tuning the JVM. We need to focus on memory functioning, latency, and throughput.

In order to monitor how our application is doing, we can use profiles. We have seen how to use the `jstat` command-line tool that comes with the JDK by default. After that, we saw how to use VisualVM to get a better visual representation of what is going on.

Next, we saw how we could adjust the heap, Metaspace, and the garbage collector of our application. We also saw the effects for our simple example application.

To reiterate, please bear in mind that adjusting the JVM to boost performance should always be the last step, and more obvious actions, such as improving code, should always be taken first.

Having covered this, you are now ready to look at how to avoid memory leaks in the next chapter.

7

Avoiding Memory Leaks

In the previous chapter, we examined how to configure and monitor memory management in the JVM. This involved knowledge of the metrics relevant to the tuning of the JVM. We discussed how to obtain these metrics and, consequently, how to tune the JVM. We also examined how to use profiling to obtain insights into the effects of tuning.

This chapter focuses on memory leaks. We will examine memory leaks under the following headings:

- Understanding memory leaks

- Spotting memory leaks

- Avoiding memory leaks

Let us start with understanding memory leaks. After that, we will learn how to spot them in our code and see how to avoid and solve them.

Technical requirements

The code for this chapter can be found on GitHub at `https://github.com/PacktPublishing/B18762_Java-Memory-Management`.

Understanding memory leaks

A memory leak occurs when objects that are no longer needed are not freed up. This causes these objects to accumulate in memory. Given that memory is a finite resource, this can eventually result in your application slowing down or even crashing (with an **out-of-memory** (**OOM**) error).

Having fast servers or hosting your application in the cloud does not abstract you from the effects of poor memory management (memory leaks). As stated earlier, memory is a finite resource and even fast servers can run out of memory. If deploying on the cloud, it is tempting to simply scale up to address the issue of memory leaks; however, this results in higher costs for deploying an instance that is larger than it needs to be. It can even lead to hefty cloud service bills.

How fast you run out of memory depends on where in your code the memory leak occurs. If this is a piece of code that seldom runs, it will take a long time for the memory to get full. However, if this is a piece of code that runs frequently, it might go a lot faster.

While the reasons for memory leaks may vary, one likely culprit is a bug in your code. This leads us to our next topic: spotting memory leaks.

Spotting memory leaks

So, you may wonder what typically when your application starts to respond somewhat slower after running for some time. The system administrator might just restart the application now and then to free the unnecessarily accumulated memory. This need for a restart is a typical symptom of a memory leak.

As memory fills up due to a memory leak, applications will slow down and even crash. While an application slowing down is not necessarily due to a memory leak, this often is the case. When faced with code that you suspect contains a memory leak, the following metrics are very helpful in diagnosing the application:

- Heap memory footprint
- Garbage collection activity
- Heap dump

In order to demonstrate how to monitor these metrics, we will need an application that contains a memory leak. *Figure 7.1* shows such a program:

```
1 package ch7;
2
3 import java.util.ArrayList;
5
6 class Person{
7     private String name;
8     Person(String aName){
9         name = aName;
10     }
11 }
12 public class OutOfMemoryExample {
13     public static void main(String[] args) {
14         List<Person> list = new ArrayList<>();
15         while(true) {
16             Person p = new Person("John");
17             list.add(p);
18         }
19     }
20
21 }
```

Figure 7.1 – Program with a memory leak

In *Figure 7.1*, we are in an infinite loop starting on *line 15*, creating `Person` objects and adding them to an `ArrayList` object. As each `Person` reference (p) is re-initialized, it is easy to think that each `Person` object that the reference previously referred to is now eligible for garbage collection. However, this is not the case, as those `Person` objects are being referred to from the `ArrayList` object and consequently cannot be reclaimed by the garbage collector. Therefore, while the infinite loop results in the program eventually running out of memory, the memory leak itself is because the garbage collector is unable to reclaim the `Person` objects. Let us examine how we can diagnose the running code to help us arrive at this conclusion.

We will run this program using the command line as we can easily specify that we want the heap dumped to a file if the heap runs out of memory. The current directory is this:

```
C:\Users\skennedy\eclipse-workspace\MemoryMgtBook\src\
```

The following command in the command line (written over several lines for clarity) achieves this:

```
java
-XX:+HeapDumpOnOutOfMemoryError
-XX:HeapDumpPath=C:\Users\skennedy\eclipse-workspace\
MemoryMgtBook\src\ch7
ch7.OutOfMemoryExample
```

The interesting parts here are the –XX options specified. In the first instance, we are turning on the `HeapDumpOnOutOfMemoryError` option. This means that if the heap runs out of memory, the JVM will dump the heap into a file. All we need to do now is specify the location and name of that file. This is what the second –XX option does, using the `HeapDumpPath` flag.

Now that we have started our memory leak-affected application, we will use the **VisualVM** application to monitor the metrics of interest. VisualVM is an application that used to come with your Java SDK, but now you'll have to download it separately from `https://visualvm.github.io/download.html` (note that this is the active link at the time of writing). Let us start with our diagnosis using the heap memory footprint.

Heap memory footprint

What we are looking for here is not the size of the heap itself, but the amount of heap *used*. We are also very interested in whether or not the garbage collector reclaims the used heap. *Figure 7.2* shows the heap footprint for the application outlined in *Figure 7.1*:

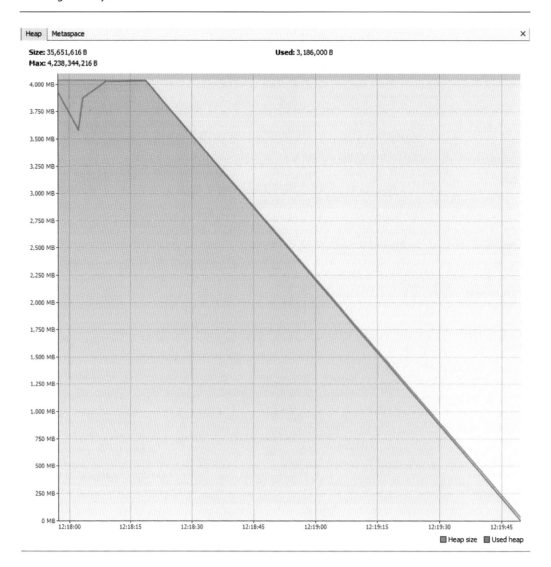

Figure 7.2 – Heap memory footprint

As can be seen from the preceding screenshot, the used heap (the area between the x axis and the graph line) quickly occupies all the heap space available. The garbage collector does manage to reclaim some memory (the dip on the left), but this is not memory allocated by our application. The program runs out of memory and crashes due to an OutOfMemoryError error. This is why the used heap goes back to 0.

Let us examine the garbage collector activity during this period.

Garbage collector activity

In the previous section, we saw the effect an application containing a memory leak has on the heap footprint. It is interesting to examine the activity of the garbage collector during that period. *Figure 7.3* reflects this:

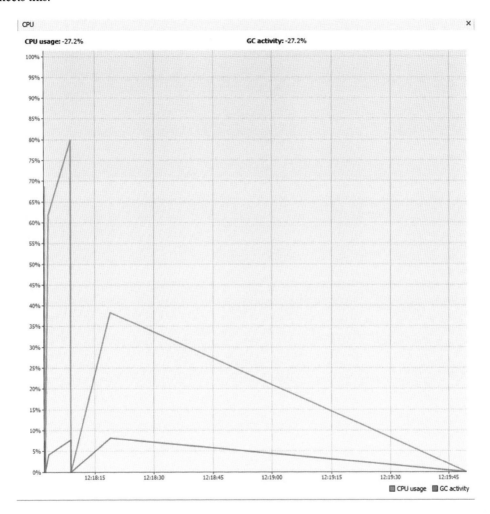

Figure 7.3 – Garbage collector activity

Figure 7.3 shows that the garbage collector is very busy during the run of the program. However, as per *Figure 7.2*, we know this had no effect on freeing up space (allocated by our application) on the heap. Thus, in spite of having a busy garbage collector, the heap remains full. This is a classic sign of a memory leak.

So now, we have validated that we have a memory leak in our program. The next step is to figure out what is causing the leak. In our case, it's rather obvious, but to help us understand better, let's investigate further. The next step would be to look at the heap dump created by the JVM when our program crashed.

Heap dump

When we ran our application, we specified that we wanted to create a heap dump if the application ran out of memory. This will enable us to further debug why we ran out of memory in the first place. *Figure 7.4* represents the heap dump summary generated:

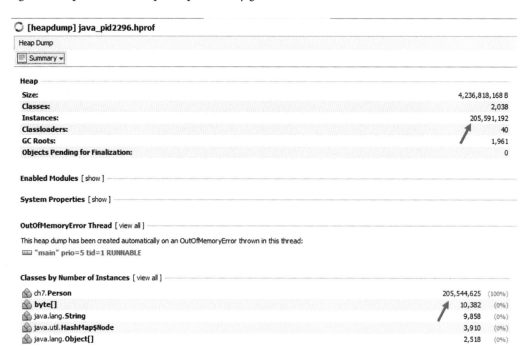

Figure 7.4 – Heap dump summary

Two values in *Figure 7.4* jump out straight away. The first is the number of *instances* (first arrow). At *205,591,192*, this is far too many. Now, we need to know what type of instance is causing the memory leak. The second red arrow highlights ch7.Person as the offending type, given that there are *205,544,625* instances of that type alone.

The heap dump also enables us to drill down further. In this case, we will do just that, as we want to see what is *preventing* the garbage collection of these Person objects. *Figure 7.5* will help us discuss that:

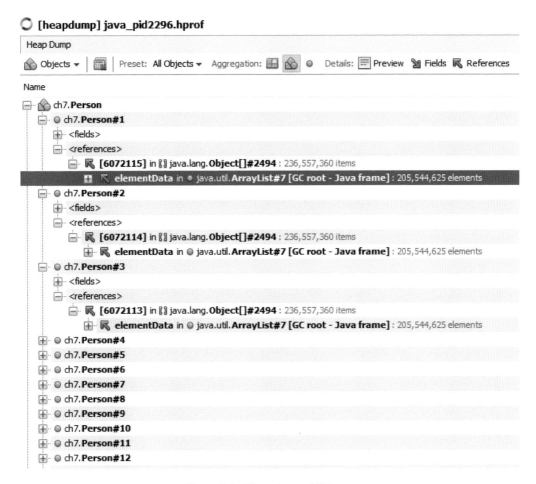

Figure 7.5 – Heap dump drilldown

In the preceding screenshot, we have drilled down from the summary level to the object level. As we know, there are a lot of Person objects. By drilling down into any one of the Person objects, we can see the type that is referring to it. As highlighted in one of the Person objects (in blue), we can see that it is an ArrayList object.

Now, we have a much clearer idea of what is happening. We are adding Person objects to an ArrayList object whose reference never goes out of scope. As a result, the garbage collector cannot remove any of these Person objects from the heap, and we end up with an OutOfMemoryError error.

To summarize, in this section, we diagnosed a program that contained a memory leak. Using the heap memory footprint and garbage collection activity, we confirmed the presence of a memory leak. We then analyzed the heap dump to ascertain the offending collection (ArrayList) and type (Person). The next section will deal with how to avoid memory leaks in the first place.

Avoiding memory leaks

The best way of avoiding a memory leak is to write code that does not contain any leaks in the first place. In other words, objects that we no longer need should *not* have connections back to the stack, as that prevents the garbage collector from reclaiming them. Before we get into techniques that help you avoid leaks in your code, let us first fix the leak presented in *Figure 7.1*. *Figure 7.6* presents the leak-free code:

```
1 package ch7;
2
3 import java.util.ArrayList;
5
6 class Person{
7     private String name;
8     Person(String aName){
9         name = aName;
10    }
11 }
12 public class OutOfMemoryExample {
13     public static void main(String[] args) {
14         List<Person> list = new ArrayList<>();
15         int i=1;
16         while(true) {
17             Person p = new Person("John");
18             list.add(p);
19             if(i == 1000) {
20                 list = new ArrayList<>();
21                 i=0;
22             }
23             i++;
24         }
25     }
26 }
```

Figure 7.6 – Leak-free program

In *Figure 7.6*, the infinite loop remains. However, *lines 19* to *23* are new. In this new section, we increment an i local variable every time we add a Person reference to the ArrayList object. Once we have done this 1,000 times, we re-initialize our list reference. This is crucial as it enables the garbage collector to reclaim the old ArrayList object and the 1,000 Person objects referred to from the ArrayList object. In addition, we reset i back to 0. This will solve the leak. (Please send us an email if you find a use case for this specific example, and we'll add it to the next edition of the book. It does, however, illustrate the example graphs well.)

We will now run the program using the same command-line arguments as before. The program does not generate an OutOfMemoryError error. We will now examine the code's performance using VisualVM. *Figure 7.6* reflects the heap memory footprint of the new memory leak-free code:

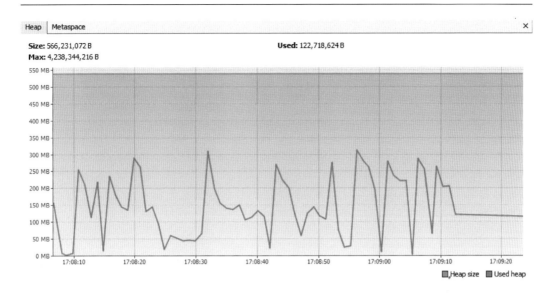

Figure 7.7 – Heap memory footprint (leak-free code)

As we can see in the preceding screenshot, the used heap space (area between the *x* axis and the graph) goes up and down. The down areas reflect where the garbage collector reclaims memory. This pattern resembles the teeth of a saw and is a sign of a healthy program. Toward the end, we stopped running the program.

Next, we will look at the garbage collector activity during that time. *Figure 7.8* reflects this:

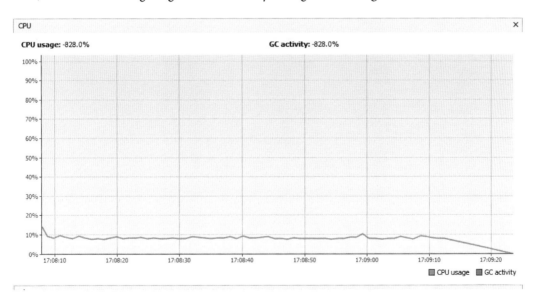

Figure 7.8 – Garbage collector activity (leak-free code)

In *Figure 7.3* (the graph representing the code with the memory leak), the garbage collector was running at over 5%. Here, in *Figure 7.8*, however, the garbage collector is barely noticeable at all and almost the same as the *x* axis. Again, a sign of a healthy program. As this program does not run out of heap space, there is no need for a heap dump.

Common pitfalls and how to avoid them

Now that we have addressed the memory leak issue, we will review some common problems in code and how to avoid them. We will discuss techniques that will enable us to write leak-free code and code that uses memory in an optimal way without wasting resources that we actually did not need to use.

Some of the tips are a bit more obvious and don't require a lot of examples, such as assigning a decent amount of heap space to your program if this is possible for the system, as well as not creating objects that you don't need and reusing objects when you can. Some of them require a little more explanation, and we'll elaborate on them next.

Unnecessary references on the stack and setting the reference to null

It is possible that there are references on the stack that are actually no longer needed. In our preceding example, this was the case.

Re-initializing the reference (or setting it to null) is the approach used in this section to fix the memory leak. Both approaches break the link back to the stack, enabling the garbage collector to reclaim the heap memory. Be careful, though, that you only do this when your application is finished with the objects; otherwise, you'll get `NullPointerException` exceptions. You can see the following example:

```
Person personObj = new Person();
// use personObj
personObj = null;
```

In this example, we're having an object reference stored in `personObj`; when we no longer need it, we set it to null. This way, the `Person` object on the heap becomes eligible for garbage collection after the line where we set it to null (assuming that we didn't assign the reference to other variables).

Whether or not this approach is still relevant for today's software is questionable; for most modern applications, this approach is less favorable, but of course, there could be sensible use cases.

Resource leaks and closing resources

When you open resources such as files, databases, streams, and so on, they take up memory. If these resources are not closed, this could lead to resource leaks. In some scenarios, it could even lead to a serious depletion of the available resources and affect the performance of your application—for example, the buffers could get full. If you are producing output—for example, writing to a file or committing to a database—not closing the resource might actually lead to incorrect persistence or writing of the data, and the data might not reach its intended destination such as an output file or a database.

Closing resources (such as file and database connections) when finished is a method to prevent this from happening. Using the `finally` block or `try-with-resources` is of great help here. The `finally` block is always executed, regardless of whether or not an exception occurs. `try-with-resources` has an in-built `finally` block to close any resources opened in the `try` section. Using the `finally` block or `try-with-resources` ensures that the resources will be closed.

Consider the following code of a regular `try-catch` block:

```
String path = "some path";
FileReader fr = null;
BufferedReader br = null;
try {
    fr = new FileReader(path);
    br = new BufferedReader(fr);
    System.out.println(br.readLine());
} catch(IOException e) {
    e.printStackTrace();
}
```

In this code snippet, we are opening a `FileReader` and a `BufferedReader` class and dealing with the checked exceptions in the `catch` block. However, we never close them. This way, they don't become eligible for garbage collection. Make sure to close them. This can be done in the `finally` block, like so:

```
String path = "some path";
FileReader fr = null;
BufferedReader br = null;
try {
    fr = new FileReader(path);
    br = new BufferedReader(fr);
    System.out.println(br.readLine());
} catch(IOException e) {
    e.printStackTrace();
}
finally {
    if(br != null) {
        br.close();
```

```
    }
    if(fr != null) {
        fr.close();
    }
}
```

The finally block executes, whether an exception occurred or not. This way, we can be sure that the resources are closed.

Since Java 7, it is more common to use the try-with-resources. At the end of the try block, it is going to call the close() method on the objects initialized in the try statement (these objects must be implementing the AutoCloseable interface). This is what the previous example would look like:

```
String path = "some path";
try (FileReader fr = new FileReader(path);
    BufferedReader br = new BufferedReader(fr)) {
                        System.out.println(br.readLine());
} catch(IOException e) {
    e.printStackTrace();
}
```

As you can see, this is much cleaner, and it prevents you from forgetting to close the resources. Therefore, using try-with-resources whenever possible is recommended.

Avoiding unnecessary String objects using StringBuilder

String objects are immutable and therefore cannot be changed after creation. In the background, your requested changes result in a new String object being created (which reflects your changes) while the original String object remains untouched.

For example, when you concatenate one String object onto another String object, you actually end up with three different objects in memory: the original String object, the String object you want to concatenate, and the new, resultant String object reflecting the result of the concatenation.

Put the String concatenation code into a loop, and many unnecessary objects are created in the background. Consider the following example:

```
String strIntToChar = "";
for(int i = 97; i < 123; i++) {
    strIntToChar += i + ": " + (char)i + "\n";
}
System.out.println(strIntToChar);
```

This is what the outputted `String` object will look like after the loop. We've omitted the middle section to not make this snippet unnecessarily lengthy:

```
97: a
98: b
99: c
... omitted middle ...
120: x
121: y
122: z
```

In this example, we are creating a lot of objects, and every intermediate `concat` step creates a new object. For example, after the first two iterations, the value of `strIntToChar` is this:

```
97: a
98: b
```

And after three iterations, it is this:

```
97: a
98: b
99: c
```

All these intermediate values are stored in a *String pool*. This is because `String` objects are *immutable*, and the String pool is used as an optimization that is working against us here.

The solution to this problem would be to use `StringBuilder`. `StringBuilder` objects are mutable. If we rewrite the previous code using `StringBuilder`, a lot fewer objects are created, since we are not creating a separate `String` object for every intermediate value. This is what the code would look like with `StringBuilder` instead:

```
StringBuilder sbIntToChar  = new StringBuilder("");
for(int i = 97; i < 123; i++) {
    sbIntToChar.append(i + ": " + (char)i + "\n");
}
System.out.println(sbIntToChar);
```

When concatenating, there won't be a new `StringBuilder` object created as the JVM manipulates the original `StringBuilder` object. As you can see, it doesn't require drastic changes to the code, but it does improve memory management a lot. Thus, when concatenating a `String` object a lot, use `StringBuilder`.

Managing memory usage by using primitives instead of wrapper classes

Wrapper classes require a lot more memory than primitives. Sometimes, you must use wrapper classes—it is not optional. In other cases, using primitives instead of wrapper types is an option. So, for example, create a local variable of type int instead of Integer.

Primitive variables occupy a small amount of memory, and if the primitive is local to a method, it is stored on the stack (which is faster to access than the heap). Wrappers, on the other hand, are class types and always result in the creation of an object on the heap. In addition, if it's possible, you should use the long and double primitives instead of BigInteger and BigDecimal. BigDecimal, in particular, is popular due to its precision in calculations. However, this precision comes at the price of requiring a lot more memory and slower calculations, so only use this class when you really need the precision.

Please note that this is not an actual memory leak that you're preventing, but rather optimizing the usage of memory by not requiring more memory than you need to achieve the goals of your application.

The problem with static collections and why to avoid this

In some situations, it can be tempting to use a static collection in a class to keep the objects in an application, especially when you are working with a Java SE-only environment and you'd like to store objects. This is something that is quite a danger to a healthy memory footprint. This is what such an example could look like:

```
public class AvoidingStaticCollections {
    public static List<Person> personList = new
        ArrayList<>();

    public static void addPerson(Person p) {
        personList.add(p);
    }
    // other code omitted
}
```

This could get quickly out of hand. The objects created cannot be garbage-collected because the static collection keeps them alive. There are a few better ways to go about this. If this is something you really feel you need, chances are you might be able to use a database instead.

If you are using a HashMap class as a static collection, chances are you can use a WeakHashMap (Java 8 onward) instead. This will have weak references for the keys (so please note this; not the values—these are held by strong references). These key references are stored as weak references in the WeakHashMap, but this will not prevent the garbage collector from removing the object from the heap. The entries in the `WeakHashMap` will be removed if the key is no longer used by the rest of the application. This means that it should be all right to lose information that is not referenced anywhere else. So, if your intention is to maintain the information in a `HashMap`, you *should not* be using a `WeakHashMap` instead. However, if you don't require the keys of your `HashMap` to be maintained on the heap if that's the only reference, it's possible that a `WeakHashMap` is an optimization for your heap usage. As always, research carefully whether this fits your requirements before implementing it.

Summary

In this chapter, we learned how to avoid memory leaks in our code. The first step was to understand that memory leaks occur when objects, when no longer needed, maintain links to the stack. This prevents the garbage collector from reclaiming them. Given that memory is a finite resource, this is never desirable. As these objects accumulate, your application slows down and eventually crashes.

One common source of memory leaks is bugs in our code. However, there are ways to debug memory leaks. In order to demonstrate how to debug leaky code, we presented a program containing a memory leak. VisualVM is a tool that enables us to monitor the metrics of interest—the heap memory footprint, garbage collection activity, and the heap dump (when we run out of heap space).

The heap footprint validated the presence of a memory leak as it showed the *used* heap space totally occupying the available heap space. In other words, objects on the heap were not reclaimed. Meanwhile, the garbage collector was, in vain, extremely busy trying to free up heap space. To figure out which type was causing the issue, we examined the heap dump. This led us to an `ArrayList` object referring to a massive number of `Person` instances.

We addressed the leaky code and, using VisualVM again, checked the heap footprint and garbage collector activity metrics. Both metrics were much healthier.

However, the best way to avoid memory leaks is not to code them in the first place. This is similar to the *prevention is better than cure* principle. With this in mind, we discussed a few common techniques used to avoid memory leaks in the first place.

That concludes the chapter. In short, we started by covering why and how memory leaks occur. We then diagnosed and fixed the code containing a memory leak. We finished by discussing what to keep in mind to prevent writing leaky code and how to optimize memory usage in the first place.

This doesn't just conclude the chapter but also the book. We started with an overview of the memory and zoomed in on the different aspects. After that, we dived into garbage collection. The last chapters of the book focused on how to improve performance: how to tune the JVM and how to avoid memory leaks.

If you'd like to know even more about how the JVM manages memory, the official documentation of the JVM is out there waiting for you. You can find the latest version here: `https://docs.oracle.com/javase/specs/index.html`.

Index

Subscribe to our online digital library for full access to over 7,000 books and videos, as well as industry leading tools to help you plan your personal development and advance your career. For more information, please visit our website.

Why subscribe?

- Spend less time learning and more time coding with practical eBooks and Videos from over 4,000 industry professionals

- Improve your learning with Skill Plans built especially for you

- Get a free eBook or video every month

- Fully searchable for easy access to vital information

- Copy and paste, print, and bookmark content

Did you know that Packt offers eBook versions of every book published, with PDF and ePub files available? You can upgrade to the eBook version at packt.com and as a print book customer, you are entitled to a discount on the eBook copy. Get in touch with us at customercare@packtpub.com for more details.

At www.packt.com, you can also read a collection of free technical articles, sign up for a range of free newsletters, and receive exclusive discounts and offers on Packt books and eBooks.

Other Books You May Enjoy

If you enjoyed this book, you may be interested in these other books by Packt:

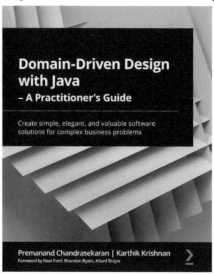

Domain-Driven Design with Java - A Practitioner's Guide

Premanand Chandrasekaran, Karthik Krishnan

ISBN: 978-1-80056-073-4

- Discover how to develop a shared understanding of the problem domain
- Establish a clear demarcation between core and peripheral systems
- Identify how to evolve and decompose complex systems into well-factored components
- Apply elaboration techniques like domain storytelling and event storming
- Implement EDA, CQRS, event sourcing, and much more
- Design an ecosystem of cohesive, loosely coupled, and distributed microservices
- Test-drive the implementation of an event-driven system in Java
- Grasp how non-functional requirements influence bounded context decompositions

Learn Java 17 Programming - Second Edition

Nick Samoylov

ISBN: 978-1-80324-143-2

- Understand and apply object-oriented principles in Java
- Explore Java design patterns and best practices to solve everyday problems
- Build user-friendly and attractive GUIs with ease
- Understand the usage of microservices with the help of practical examples
- Discover techniques and idioms for writing high-quality Java code
- Get to grips with the usage of data structures in Java

Packt is searching for authors like you

If you're interested in becoming an author for Packt, please visit `authors.packtpub.com` and apply today. We have worked with thousands of developers and tech professionals, just like you, to help them share their insight with the global tech community. You can make a general application, apply for a specific hot topic that we are recruiting an author for, or submit your own idea.

Share Your Thoughts

Now you've finished *Java Memory Management*, we'd love to hear your thoughts! Scan the QR code below to go straight to the Amazon review page for this book and share your feedback or leave a review on the site that you purchased it from.

`https://packt.link/r/1801812853`

Your review is important to us and the tech community and will help us make sure we're delivering excellent quality content.

Download a Free PDF copy of this book

Thanks for purchasing this book!

Do you like to read on the go but are unable to carry your print books everywhere?

Is your eBook purchase not compatible with the device of your choice?

Don't worry, now with every Packt book you get a DRM-free PDF version of that book at no cost.

Read anywhere, any place, on any device. Search, copy, and paste code from your favorite technical books directly into your application.

The perks don't stop there, you can get exclusive access to discounts, newsletters, and great free content in your inbox daily

Follow these simple steps to get the benefits:

1. Scan the QR code or visit the link below

https://packt.link/free-ebook/9781801812856

2. Submit your proof of purchase
3. That's it! We'll send your free PDF and other benefits to your email directly

Printed in Great Britain
by Amazon